Cambridge Elements ≡

Elements in Public Policy
edited by
M. Ramesh
National University of Singapore
Michael Howlett
National University of Singapore
David L. Weimar
University of Wisconsin – Madison
Xun Wu
Hong Kong University of Science and Technology
Judith Clifton
University of Cantabria
Eduardo Araral
National University of Singapore

DESIGNING FOR POLICY EFFECTIVENESS

Defining and Understanding a Concept

B. Guy Peters
University of Pittsburgh
Giliberto Capano
University of Bologna
Michael Howlett
National University of Singapore
Ishani Mukherjee
National University of Singapore
Meng-Hsuan Chou
Nanyang Technological University, Singapore
Pauline Ravinet
Université de Lille

CAMBRIDGE
UNIVERSITY PRESS

CAMBRIDGE
UNIVERSITY PRESS

University Printing House, Cambridge CB2 8BS, United Kingdom

One Liberty Plaza, 20th Floor, New York, NY 10006, USA

477 Williamstown Road, Port Melbourne, VIC 3207, Australia

314–321, 3rd Floor, Plot 3, Splendor Forum, Jasola District Centre, New Delhi – 110025, India

79 Anson Road, #06–04/06, Singapore 079906

Cambridge University Press is part of the University of Cambridge.

It furthers the University's mission by disseminating knowledge in the pursuit of education, learning, and research at the highest international levels of excellence.

www.cambridge.org
Information on this title: www.cambridge.org/9781108453110
DOI: 10.1017/9781108555081

First published 2018

A catalogue record for this publication is available from the British Library.

ISBN 978-1-108-45311-0 Paperback
ISSN 2398-4058 (online)
ISSN 2514-3565 (print)

Cambridge Elements ☰

Designing for Policy Effectiveness

Abstract: *Policy studies has always been interested in analyzing and improving upon the sets of policy tools adopted by governments to correct policy problems. In order to do so, policy studies emphasizes better understanding, and improving the processes, of policy analysis and policy formulation. Past scholarly work has helped clarify the role of historical processes, policy capacities, and design intentions in affecting policy formulation processes and policy designs, and more recently in understanding how the bundling of multiple policy elements to meet policy goals can be better understood and done. Although this work has progressed, the discussion of the overall goals that policy designs should serve remains disjointed. Here it is argued that a central goal – in fact, the central goal – of policy design is effectiveness. Effectiveness serves as the basic goal of any design, upon which other goals, such as efficiency and equity, are built.*

Keywords: policy design, policy formulation capacity

ISSNs: 2398-4058 (online) 2514-3565 (print)

ISBNs: 9781108453110 (PB) 9781108555081 (OC)

---

1 The Evolution of Design Thinking: When Did Effectiveness Take Center Stage ... and Has It?

The essence of policy design resides in the articulation of policy options to meet government goals. Not all policies are as well or as

Meng-Hsuan Chou and Pauline Ravinet acknowledge the funding support from the Ministry of Education of Singapore (AcRF Tier 1) to help undertake research for this Element.

1

carefully formulated as they could be, and policy studies has been interested for several decades in understanding questions such as why some policy alternatives are developed and others are not, why some are successfully adopted while others are not, and how some policies emerge from carefully crafted formulation processes while others become more heavily influenced by processes such as political, partisan, or electoral or legislative bargaining (Howlett, 2011). Why design occurs and how superior designs can be achieved in complex issue-areas are outstanding topics in contemporary formulation studies (Howlett, 2014a; Howlett et al., 2015).

How to best design public policies has always been a central concern of contemporary public policy analysis and has recently come back into focus owing to a new wave of policy design thinking. This question, like many in the social sciences, has followed a cyclical pattern of interest and has attracted work from several different perspectives over the past several decades. Some of the founders of the field of policy sciences, including Harold Lasswell, for example, were already discussing policy design, but perhaps like Monsieur Jourdain and proselytes, they did not know it at the time and did not follow up systematically on this interest. Lasswell's notion of policy analysis being "social engineering" (1951) clearly has a design element, given that engineers and architects are often cited as clear examples of professions with a strong design component. The term "design" was used infrequently in these earlier discussions, and there was little attempt to then think of policy analysis as design.

In the late 1970s into the 1980s there was a second wave of studies following a burst of enthusiasm about the state's capacity to design programs to meet perceived policy problems in this era (see Alexander,1982; Dryzek, 1983; Linder & Peters, 1984, 1991; Bobrow & Dryzek, 1987).[1] In seeking more efficient and better solutions to implementation and other problems which were

[1] Interestingly, this spate of interest in design occurred shortly after Horst Rittel and Melvin Webber (1973) had declared that the problems facing governments were "wicked," and Herbert Simon (1973) was emphasizing the nature of ill-structured problems. Both of those characterizations of policy problems are

seen to have plagued policy initiatives of the 1960s and 1970s (Pressman & Wildavsky, 1973), these discussions of design attempted to identify ways of designing interventions that could "work" and would "solve" problems, notwithstanding and overcoming the many barriers to successful policymaking identified in these works.

Overtaken by events such as the election of neoliberal and neoconservative governments in the 1970s and 1980s, who believed strongly in nonstate, market-based solutions to many problems, the interest in design became largely dormant in the field for the next two decades, with the very notable exceptions of the works of Anne Schneider and Helen Ingram (1997) and some colleagues such as David Weimer (1992, 1993) and Peter de Leon (1997), who focused on the political nature and consequences of design choices, including how different design "targets" were identified and characterized as either deserving or undeserving of state action, whether or not they were treated in either a benign or maligned fashion, and how policy advisors and decision-makers approached these issues. Although often forgotten in discussions of policy design that are focused more on problem solving and developing effective policies (see Section 2), this version of design placed the "publicness" of public policy at the center of the analysis. This is true for public policies as both the *consequences* of democratic decision-making, as well as the role of public policy in *facilitating* democracy and democratic practices.

In general, however, this work does not focus on specific design practices and principles and how these could be more clearly articulated and expounded to draw out lessons or best practices for erstwhile designers. These subjects have been a major orientation and research object in the most recent rebirth of interest in policy design in the last decade, which is the main subject of this Element.

---

antithetical to naive notions of design, especially those that assume that one could develop an algorithm to map solutions onto problems.

Policy design is a process which falls on the more purposive and instrumental end of the formulation spectrum but entails the same issues of feasibility and acceptance. That is, it involves the deliberate endeavor to link policy tools with clearly articulated policy goals (Majone, 1975; Linder & Peters, 1984; May, 2003; Bobrow, 2006) and is based on the systematic effort to analyze the impacts of policy instruments on policy targets. Policy design is also about the application of this knowledge to the creation and realization of policies that can reasonably be expected to attain anticipated policy outcomes (Bobrow & Dryzek, 1987; Sidney, 2007; Weaver, 2009a, 2009b; Gilabert & Lawford-Smith, 2012). Such activities, however, assume that alternatives, which are feasible to realizable, will be generated through formulation and design processes and that such alternatives will emerge triumphant in deliberations and conflicts involved in these activities.

Although the contemporary version of policy design returns to some themes found in earlier studies, the optimism of earlier writings has been tempered by an appropriate concern for the difficulty of policy problems, including those considered relatively simple compared to the contemporary interest in wicked problems (Head, 2016). While academics from diverse fields such as architecture and computer design to public policy (Bason, 2014) remain very optimistic about designing innovative solutions to public problems, the enthusiasm of policy scholars has been moderated by past experience. Public policy scholars recognize the high degree of difficulty that is involved in making democratic forms of governance work effectively in addressing social problems whose very definitions and solutions are typically highly charged and contested, and linked closely to prevailing ideologies and electoral considerations.[2]

This Element discusses in greater detail this background to the study of policy design in the policy sciences, and directly addresses

---

[2] This is a statement not just about the deadlocks in American government but also some of the apparent malaise in other democratic regimes, such as the European Union, as well.

the role of the concept of "effectiveness" in the most recent round of development of design thinking in policy studies. The first argument is that, although not done explicitly, there has always been some concern with achieving effectiveness and efficiency in policy designs. That said, there is also a second strand of thinking that emphasizes more political and participatory elements in design, and which tends to be less concerned with efficiency than with democratic values, including efficiency.[3]

2   The Development of Policy Design Thinking

Policy studies has always been interested in analyzing and improving upon the sets of policy tools adopted by governments to correct policy problems, and to acquire a better understanding of how to improve processes of policy analysis and formulation in order to do so. Past studies have helped to clarify the role of historical policy choices, existing policy capacities, and present design intentions in affecting policy formulation processes and policy designs. More recently, design studies have been involved in understanding how the bundling of multiple policy elements to meet policy goals can be carried out in a better fashion. Although this work has progressed, the discussion of the overall goals that policy designs should serve remains disjointed. A central goal – in fact, *the* central goal – of policy design is "effectiveness." Effectiveness serves as the basic foundation of any design, upon which other goals such as efficiency and equity are constructed.

The following discusses the three stages of evolution in policy design thinking and how this thinking has always emphasized efficiency and effectiveness. As will be pointed out, however, the tendency to separate effectiveness and the participatory elements

---

[3] Some years ago, the *Washington Monthly* ran a column comparing two evaluations of a single public program conducted by two different schools of public policy. One, using more economic instruments emphasizing costs and benefits, found the program to be a failure. The other, emphasizing involvement and citizen evaluations, found it to be a great success. This dualism continues to characterize policy analysis and may become more divisive.

of design has become less accentuated toward the present-day (third) stage of the policy design orientation.

2.1   Design as the Core of Policy Analysis

The earliest stage in policy design thinking argued implicitly that better design was the ultimate objective of policy analysis and the broader policy sciences. The primary goal of this initial phase of the design perspective was to understand what would be required for a functional policy design and how it could be implemented. A second goal of this era was to understand how that designing process would fit with existing literatures in the policy sciences specifically, and in the social sciences more generally. While policy analysis almost inherently involves some concern for the application of knowledge, this initial foray into thinking about policy design did not explicitly articulate how knowledge can be used to select the appropriate instruments for the tasks at hand, but rather dealt more generally with issues around knowledge utilization in government (Weiss 1976; Caplan & Weiss 1977, Whiteman 1985a, 1985b).

These initial stages of a more explicit application of design thinking to policymaking adopted a clearer perspective on policy that relied upon analogies between policy design and the practices found in older design disciplines such as engineering and architecture. As such, it moved policy analysis away from normal patterns of thinking in the social sciences, at least to some degree, which emphasized inductive analysis and careful theory construction based on observation and analysis (Dryzek, 1983). There was some tendency for the initial versions of design to appear almost technocratic, assuming a highly mechanical ("cookbook") process for choosing policy alternatives. This conception was also more top-down than other extant approaches to policymaking, suggesting that some "designer" would develop a synoptic design and subsequently implement that design in much the same way as an architect might conceive and execute a building. This clashed with other approaches which emphasized the roles played by many lower-level participants in policymaking, from lobbyists and the public, in affecting and informing the work and decisions made by high-level executives and administrators (Shore et al., 2011; Turnbull 2017).

Nevertheless, in the second wave of policy design studies, authors such as Stephen Linder and Guy Peters (1987, 1991) argued that policy design was possible and common, and could be understood through identifying three very fundamental characteristics of the policy process and policy practice. The first was having a model of causation: We have a policy problem and how did it emerge? What is the causal mechanism that lies behind the appearance of the problem? The more technocratic version of design often assumed that there is *a* cause, whereas Linder and Peters suggested that a more political conception of the same issue was needed which would assume that there are *multiple* potential models of causation.

The second dimension of policy design was about having a model of instrumentation during formulation: How can governments intervene in an ongoing policy process to produce some desired movement toward the attainment of government aims on the part of the targets of the policy (Lascoumes & Legales, 2007)? There is a vast literature now on policy instruments, with multiple classifications and taxonomies (Howlett, 2011), but what was required was an analytical perspective that could map the available instruments onto the characteristics of the problems and targets in such a way that would guarantee a high probability of stated aims getting accomplished. The search for such an algorithm was a central element of this second, and generally technocratic, perspective on policy design.

The third element of policy design that was identified was a concern for values during policy evaluation. This feature rescued design from being a purely technocratic exercise since highlighting the normative aspects of evaluation would help avoid moves toward developing "good designs for bad policies." In other words, it would address concerns about developing workable designs for immoral, unethical, or illegal aims and ambitions that governments might have. Similar to the notions of causation, this element acknowledged that there could be multiple alternative value systems used for evaluation and also encouraged their application. While it is true that economic values of maximizing utility tend to dominate in most policy analytics and heavily influenced design in this direction (Tribe, 1972; Banfield, 1977), alternative values of participation, interactions, and ethics can also be used to assess the success or failure of public programs (Hawkesworth, 1992).

This second wave perspective on design was a challenge to several of the prevailing ideas about policymaking at the time, notably incrementalism and bounded rationality (see Peters, 1988), which were both anti-planning and anti-design in the sense used here. That is, in both of these familiar approaches to policymaking there is an assumption that designing is almost inherently misguided, given the likelihood of getting the design wrong and imposing additional costs for redoing the policy (see Hayes, 2006). The assumption was, and remains among advocates of these approaches, that the environments into which policies were being interjected were so complex and had so many actors that it was well nigh impossible for any synoptic solution to be effective.

It should also be made clear that in this stage of policy design, thinking was far from homogenous on this score. Some scholars such as Davis Bobrow and John Dryzek, for example, were interested in policy design and acknowledged its prevalence but were more skeptical about the possibilities and difficulties involved in successful design. They pointed to the variety of different theoretical perspectives that could be brought to bear on the design issue, and how those different perspectives might produce very different guidance to decision-makers and the public concerning what would constitute "good" designs.

Other approaches, however, forged ahead with fewer concerns about the challenges of design, assuming that, with the application of sufficient analytic energy, these problems could be overcome.

A close analysis of this stage of policy design thinking shows it was very much concerned with the effectiveness of public programs. The language used at this time was more about problem solving than about effectiveness per se, but the underlying logic and intention of the analysis was very much the same. Renate Mayntz (1983) usefully codified this concern, arguing that many of the fundamental issues raised by the second stage of policy design studies revolved around this issue, including concerns with the ambiguous definition of policy effectiveness, the relevance of the choice of policy instruments, the strength of values in designing policies, and the fact that policy design is channeled by structural and contextual conditions.

In contrast to other forms of policy analysis, such as cost-benefit analysis, the discussion of designing in this second phase did not focus on relative degrees of effectiveness of alternative interventions to any significant degree. Rather, it focused on the capacity to link solutions to problems in a somewhat more abstract manner and assumed that any solution that emerged from the process would, almost by definition, be effective. Perhaps from hubris or the failure to include sufficiently possible (probable) political contestation about alternative designs, the focus primarily was on finding a single design or single tool choice which could fully resolve a policy problem or difficulty.[4]

2.2　The Third (Present) Stage of Design

There was a period of quiescence after this flurry of interest in policy design. This may be a result of academic fad and fashion, but it also reflected the difficulties encountered in the real world of actually applying the design logics that had been created, and in

---

[4] That said, these analyses did recognize that there would be multiple models of causation that would in turn produce alternative designs. But the assumption appears to have been that prior to any design activity, some model of causation would have been selected. The means of that selection was not, however, clearly specified.

many cases, the impossibility of finding a single tool or design which could resolve an issue. Even from our contemporary vantage point, the world at the time proved to be a difficult place where designs often did not work in the way in which they were intended, and continuous replacement and reconfiguring became commonplace in the policymaking process, moving discussion and analysis away from "design" and toward the "incremental" adjustment camp.

Difficulties with design thinking (Howlett, 2014b) also reflected the emerging complexity of service delivery in contemporary public sectors as service delivery increasingly spanned across both the public and the private sectors, involving complicated interactions among a number of public and private actors. These policy patterns are analogous to "implementation structures" identified in the public administration literature and needed to be incorporated into modern policy design thinking (Hjern & Porter, 1981; Peters, 2014).

It soon became apparent that a significant difficulty arising in the second wave of design thinking was that it focused too much on the design of implementation structures to the detriment of the design of other aspects of the policy process. Certainly, thinking about how policies can be put into effect is important. However, like the backward mapping school of implementation, there is a danger that policy choices would be shaped by implementation possibilities, rather than vice versa.

The revival of design thinking which is now occurring has been more skeptical than the initial rounds that assumed problems were indeed solvable, and that the world was relatively "tame" in the sense that problems and their causes and solutions were either well known or could be quickly ferreted out. At the same time, the sanguine perspective of the initial rounds of design thinking remained, even after the recognition of the growing importance of wicked problems and the public sector's need to confront deep-seated issues such as poverty and environmental degradation. The emphasis on needing to deal better with difficult problems and multiple actors and considerations in order to move beyond the limitations of the second round of design thinking persists to this day, and to some extent has even increased in importance.[5]

2.3　*Five Emerging Design Patterns in the Third Wave of Design Studies*

The revival in thinking about policy design in recent years has led to several attempts to reactivate designing as a central activity in policy analysis. As with many revivals of interest, different participants recall different things from the past and see different deficiencies in past practices that require rethinking and reformulation. The following describes five emerging strands of design thinking in contemporary policy studies, with each strand implying a somewhat different future about public policymaking and the relevance and possibility of policy design. With the possible exception of the first strand, these emerging trajectories of design thinking have all been influenced by the growing interest in how difficult it is to introduce effective policy interventions and underscore the need for greater clarification of this important criteria for design evaluation (Levin et al., 2012).

2.3.1　Path Dependency

The simplest pattern of development in policymaking and policy design thinking is to continue what has been done in the past. This implies a continuing interest in furthering technocratic approaches to design based on earlier thinking about target compliance and actor motivations, even with the realization of the number and type of wicked and complex problems facing governments and policy designers. At the same time in third-wave studies the language in this path-dependent version of policy design thinking has

---

[5] Indeed, the danger has become that everything that is not a simple administrative matter becomes defined as a wicked problem. This is true even though when asked most scholars do not appear to think that the attributes of wicked problems as initially articulated actually apply to many problems, even ones usually thought to be archetypical wicked problems such as climate change (see Peters & Tarpley, 2016).

changed: it is now more open to participatory methods than some of the earlier approaches even though many of the fundamental perspectives on design persist. In particular, this perspective on design continues to place the continuing effectiveness of earlier regimes and instrument, and to a lesser extent efficiency, in a central position in policy analysis.

The path-dependent approach to policy design has also been influenced by developments in the allied discipline of public administration. The spread of the New Public Management, and market thinking in general in the public sector, has emphasized effectiveness and efficiency in the implementation of public programs, and those values have dominated the design of programs as well as their implementation under such rubrics (Barzelay, 2001). This approach to policy shares some of the technocratic elements associated with earlier design thinking, which assumed that management science could provide guidance for implementation, and to some extent formulation, of programs in a neutral nonpartisan way.[6]

Interestingly, the path-dependent approach to design often returns design thinking to the realms of incrementalism and bounded rationality. Fundamentally, doing what one has always done does indeed provide some guarantee of a minimal level (status quo) of effectiveness. Unless a program has been an abject failure, its persistence will mean the continuation of some level of effective service for clients. However, the (significant) advances in efficiency or effectiveness that other forms of design might offer remain out of reach.

At the same time, saying that designing may be path dependent does not imply that changes cannot take place; rather, it means that change may be driven less by agency and purposeful action than by bureaucratic regimes and standard operating practices, among other factors. It may also mean, however, that policy change will be driven less by hubris than by political interactions

---

[6] There are some elements of "backward mapping" (Elmore, 1985) involved here. The market ideas from implementation are used to help shape, if not determine, the design of the program to be implemented. This has been most true of the choice of market-based policy instruments.

among the multiple participants involved in the process of making and implementing policy, as Charles Lindblom (1959) suggested, in his early work on incrementalism and its penchant for marginal adjustment to the status quo.

2.3.2 Diffusion as Design

Much of the first- and second-generation policy design literature appears to have assumed that design occurred as a *tabula rasa,* in which a completely new policy was developed from scratch and put into place, often after an older one had been scrapped. But the simplest way to design a program is to copy another, existing policy. This practice, highlighted in the academic study of policy diffusion, is hardly a novel occurrence, but in the contemporary period there has been increased interest in learning from innovations in other governments and studying this learning more systematically.

This is sometimes done for technical reasons – to see "what works" and where with respect to specific tool deployments and designs – but there is also often a political aspect in that successful practice in some other jurisdiction can provide a good deal of protection for politicians who advocate policy reforms, helping them to avoid blame for any failure or to claim credit for success, as the case may be (Hood, 2002; Mesequer, 2006). Moreover, direct copying can also reduce the time and expense involved in designing and field-testing a new intervention.

Although diffusion is an inexpensive means of designing, or rather using policy designs, it is less clear that it is as capable of producing effective policies as its advocates might have us believe. The simpler and more technical the issue is, the more likely diffusion is to be effective, and the more likely that evidence from one setting can be carried over to another. However, for the major challenges facing most policymaking systems, diffusion may encounter a number of important social, cultural, and political barriers (Pritchett & Woolcock 2004). What we have then is two extremes: while the more technocratic advocates of design simply assume that good ideas would triumph, others remain skeptical and suggest that mindless emulation may result.

2.3.3 Evidence-Based Policymaking

The diffusion of policy designs has also intensified interest in policy design studies of the practices and pitfalls of evidence-based policymaking or the application of knowledge about tools and designs to policy decisions (Pawson, 2006). While most policy-makers think that they have been involved in evidence-based policymaking for their entire careers, this catchphrase about pol-icymaking reflects an effort on the part of government policy-makers and critics alike to inject into decision-making more knowledge and information and less ideology and partisanship (see Botterill & Hindmoor, 2012). Several national governments have embarked on major efforts to enhance the use of available evidence in their policymaking, although some policy areas – health and medicine in particular – appear to have been more successful than others (see Sackett et al., 1996).[7]

The use of evidence-based policymaking has also emphasized effectiveness as a key criterion in evaluating policy design. The reason for copying programs from other jurisdictions, or per-haps more commonly, gathering evidence from a number of pro-grams, is that the information collected provides evidence about programs that appear to "work" and those that don't. "Working" in this sense is often defined rather narrowly in terms of reaching specific targets and goals, and may ignore many of the secondary and tertiary consequences of the programs in question, let alone the manner in which, and by whom, evidence is collected, stored, and disseminated, which may well bias results in particular direc-tions. It is a minimalist version of effectiveness, albeit still a concern about effectiveness.

---

[7] That said, the diffusion of ideas about specific forms of medical service has been more effective than the ideas about the social aspects of medicine, given the importance of cultural understandings in "health" as opposed to medicine.

2.3.4 Actor-Centered Designing

A third emerging aspect of contemporary design thinking moves it from the passive voice toward the active voice. While identifying the exceptions is extremely easy, much of the earlier design literature had not been clear about who the "designer" was and the role of individuals and individual behavior in producing these designs. There may have been some notion that very clever policy analysis would be involved in this process, or in the case of democratic designing that it would be participatory, but this emphasis was rather vague in many cases. Similarly, even the work of Schneider and Ingram (1997) which focused on design behavior did not provide many insights into who, exactly, it was that carried stereotypical and prejudicial views of policy "targets" into policy design activities.

Mark Considine and his colleagues (2009, 2014), however, have advanced the agent-centered approach to design and to policy formulation more generally (see also Jordan & Turnpenny, 2016), which has been very useful in helping to close this gap in knowledge. This emphasis on the role of the designer and a conceptualization of design as a craft is to some extent the antithesis of the more technocratic approach previously described and harkens back to the work of David Weimer in the early days of policy design studies (Weimer, 1992). The technocratic approach assumes that an algorithm can be identified and applied to a range of cases. The craft approach, on the other hand, highlights the unique characteristics of each decision situation and how the experience and implicit knowledge of designers are utilized to produce the policy designs.[8]

Reflecting what Hal Colebatch (2017) has termed "authoritative instrumentalism," this approach to policy design places the emphasis in designing on the role of political leaders. In so doing, it assigns permanent civil servants, policy advisors, and

---

[8] The "craft" characterization also harkens back to James Thompson and Arthur Tuden (1959) typology of types of problems and decision-making in public administration.

those who usually are associated with policy formulation to a less important role in the design process (but see Page, 2012), and reduces the public and nongovernmental actors to an even more subordinate position. This raises a number of questions, not about the capacity of typically short-term and generalist ministers to be effective designers in complex policy areas requiring specialized knowledge and experience only gatherable over a long period of time (Hallerberg & Wehner, 2013), but about how ministers use available policy advice and how such advice is organized into policy advisory systems in order to supplement their own knowledge and help them reach their decisions (Seymour-Ure, 1987; Barker & Peters, 1993).

Analytically it is very important to consider agency more carefully in the design process. Considine et al. (2009, 2014) appear very sanguine about the policy capacity of ministers, but existing evidence challenges this prospect. As already noted, this opens up the consideration of issues of policy advice and the manner in which a range of actors involved in the process interact to generate designs (Halligan, 1995; Craft & Howlett, 2012). As Considine et al. note, assessing the relative effectiveness of designs that are generated through different processes involving different actors forms a significant research agenda for the new policy design studies.

2.3.5 Coping with Wickedness Directly

Another aspect of policy design studies emerging in the past several years reflects analytic, and to some extent practical, attempts to cope with "wicked" or "messy" problems. As noted earlier, the revival of the notion of wicked problems as a focus for analysis has in earlier times dampened optimism about the capacity to design. At the same time, however, this revival has emphasized the necessity to think more creatively about how to intervene into these difficult situations (Verweij, 2011). Although the characteristics of wicked problems are in many instances antithetical to designing interventions (e.g., the absence of a stopping rule or even of clear definitions of the problem), the severity of these issues demands action (Newman & Head, 2017).

Many problems confronting contemporary policy designers are difficult, if not formally wicked (see Peters & Tarpley, 2016), in the sense that problem causes and potential solutions may be known. However, they may also be "superwicked" (Levin et al., 2012) in the sense that not only are these unknowns present, but there may be time constraints and other limitations on gathering information and learning.

Conceptualizing the nature of the problems and understanding the difficulties they present for designing is thus even more important in these settings than it is for more "tame" policy problems. The wickedness of many contemporary policy problems will, in turn, also contribute to a movement away from more technocratic forms of intervention in favor of more process-oriented versions of design, as will be described in the following sections.

2.3.6   Emerging Design Thinking from Other Fields and Disciplines

While the earlier thinking about policy design was wedded to a rather mechanistic and technocratic form of thinking, and current work in the policy sciences remains heavily influenced by this intellectual debt and current, emerging ideas about design stemming from other design sciences may lead us down very different pathways of thinking about policy design process, and about their products. Indeed, at the most extreme the process may be the product, with building mechanisms for constant thinking and reform becoming institutionalized as a mechanism for making and implementing policies. Thus, in a significantly less technocratic perspective on the subject, the process of designing becomes the design in a process sometimes referred to as "co-design" (Lee, 2008).

The preceding description may appear to be word play, but it is not. Rather, it is an attempt to point to the indeterminacy of some contemporary thinking about design, and the need to consider it more fully, as a remedy for hubris if nothing else, in all its aspects, from aim and goals to participants and actors. For many practitioners and scholars alike, the notion of arriving at a definite solution for a policy problem of any significance appears increasingly infeasible. Thus, where we are in policy design may reflect Ted Lowi's notion (1972) of the importance of affecting the policy environment rather than affecting (or effecting) the policy itself. That is, by attempting to shape, and to first understand, the conditions under which policies must be made may have a more enduring effect than any one intervention, and designing policies with robust processes rather than robust contents may be the order of the day (Capano & Woo, 2017; Capano et al., forthcoming).

This less determinate perspective on design also reflects the recognition of the difficulties encountered in many policy areas with finding definitive solutions to increasingly complex problems. Following the more systemic logic, this version of designing suggests that any individual policy is itself impacted by, and impacts, other policies. Phrased differently, it is a component of a *problematique* (Warfield & Perino Jr., 1999) rather than necessarily a freestanding policy.[9] This embedded nature of policies in turn requires understanding better how policies are linked together and how they cohere, or fail to be integrated (Howlett et al., 2017). It further involves designing interventions that address the linkages and interactions among policies, even those policies not necessarily within the same domain. These interventions may need to go beyond conventional coordination (Peters, 2017) or policy integration (Jordan & Lenschow, 2010) to address more fundamental linkages among policies and policy domains.

To date the research emphasis on policy design as a problematic and often conflict-laden process of policy formulation has focused on questions such as those exploring the tradeoffs and interactions between the various tools of governance used in policy "toolkits," and the need to manage their inherent complementarities as well as contradictions and overlaps (Gunningham et al., 1998; Howlett, 2014b; Howlett et al., 2015). Studies have emphasized factors such as the different processes and patterns through which policy

---

[9] The May and Jochim concept of policy regime (2013) bears some similarities to the structural connections among policies assumed in this approach to policy design.

toolkits have developed over time by being layered on past design decisions (Thelen, 2004; Howlett & Rayner, 2013) as often resulting in less "rational" mixes of policy tools than might have been originally desired or planned.

This focus on policy mixes, layering, and temporality differentiates the existing design literature from earlier approaches that examined aspects of policymaking and especially policy tool selection by concentrating on simple policy contexts and the selection of singular tools (Salamon, 1989; Linder & Peters, 1990; del Río & Howlett, 2013). However, this different focus, while adding an important set of new dimensions to the issues of "who designs what, when and how" (Howlett, 2014b) has also somewhat overshadowed the integration of "best practices" studies into formal policy design theory and thinking. That is, this approach to understanding and making public policy should integrate not only a solid understanding of policy processes but also a deep understanding of the characteristics of policy tools and how they operate both singly and in tandem with others conjointly.

3 Effectiveness in Policy Design: What Is It? How Do We Get There? Why Do We Want It?

This emerging version of thinking about policy design to some extent returns to the more democratic thinking about design associated with Schneider and Ingram, and with de Leon (1997). Rather than relying on expertise and imposition, the emerging thinking about policy design tends to focus more on inclusion and dialogue about policy. As with other deliberative and dialogical models of policy, however, it faces difficulties in integrating information and knowledge about policies with how to derive the range of potential policy interventions.

In this latest version of policy design, *effectiveness* takes on a somewhat different definition and importance than it has in the past. Here, designing effectiveness is defined less as the achievement of specific policy targets and more in terms of creating a frame for action that may shape a range of policy responses

(Latour, 2008). The frame can be used to define problems and to provide some options for addressing those problems.

By emphasizing the embedded nature of policy problems, perhaps even more so than the wicked problems framework, this almost inevitably focuses attention on the need for integration of solutions across a range of concerns and raises the issue of the problematic relationship between effectiveness as achievement of a specific result and effectiveness as legitimation of the process through which problem, process, and result are collectively defined and accepted.

That is, policy design is about finding effective solutions to policy problems, but it is also about other aspects of policy. Effectiveness for policies is always a relative term, with aspirations for, and assumptions about, the effectiveness of an intervention being dependent upon a number of factors. While the expectations of being able to achieve efficiency through relatively simple design interventions now appear at best optimistic, there still is a sense that, with attention to process as well as content, designers may be able to craft policies that can at least address policy problems with a high(er) degree of effectiveness.

In other words, experience from a variety of sectors and jurisdictions have alluded to different aspects of what constitutes *effectiveness* or *best practices* in the activity of policy design but less so about what constitutes a good or effective design. Discussion of this latter topic is a largely scattered body of knowledge in policy studies, presenting a significant opportunity to draw lessons on what "effectiveness" means for the multiple levels of design, ranging from abstract policy goals and instrument logics that inform the policy design environment, to the more specific mechanics of policy programs and toolkits that match particular policy objectives to individual tool settings.

3.1 What Is Policy Effectiveness?

Effectiveness, in the context of policy design, can be understood at three levels of analysis. The first is at the level of broad indication of what entails an effective formulation environment or *spaces* that are conducive to effective design. The second and related issue concerns how effective policy tool portfolios or mixes can be effectively constructed to address complex policy goals; that is, what is an effective policy design *process*? And the third entails a more specific focus on what accounts for and constitutes the effectiveness of particular types of policy *tools*. Whereas the existing policy design literature has begun to look at the first two of these levels of understanding, the third was the subject of older studies which can be resurrected and incorporated with the others.

3.1.1 The Role of Design Spaces: Defining Effective Design Environments

By the late 1990s, policy design scholars had begun to progress from the study of single instrument uses to the analysis of more complex policy mixes (Grabosky, 1994; Gunningham et al., 1998; Howlett, 2004). This era also saw a substantial shift in scholarly attention toward more "meta" level studies of policy governance, sparked by the emergence of globalization and its preference for market-based tools as well as the start of "governance" studies undertaken in Europe and elsewhere which emphasized the role of nonstate actors, especially networks, in policymaking (Howlett & Lejano, 2012). This "globalization and governance turn" encouraged a polarization of discussions about effectiveness in design at a very abstract level such as that between instruments of the "market" and the "state," or between dichotomous governance styles such as "hierarchies" and "markets" (Howlett, 2004; Koch, 2013).

This often led to fairly simple design precepts about what constitutes effective policymaking being put forward by students of globalization and governance, such as an absolute preference for market-based tools or collaborative governance arrangements at all times (Hay & Smith, 2010; Jarvis, 2011; Tollefson et al., 2012). These studies were undoubtedly biased but still useful in helping to link policy design thinking and studies to work on policy styles and other such "meta" governance activities. However, a wider vocabulary of tools and instruments is needed if effective programs and choices are to be elaborated and adopted (Hood, 2007; Hood & Margetts, 2007).

Importantly, though, this orientation also raised questions about the environment of "spaces" in which formulation processes occur both at this "meta" and at the more specific level of policy tools to generate outcomes or designs, and whether or not certain kinds of spaces were more likely to produce better results than others.

The idea, of course, is that the nature of the overall policy design space can have a significant bearing on how effectively intended design activities take place and thus upon the likely effectiveness of policy designs which emerge from them. As early as 1991, Linder and Peters had suggested that policy design could be thought of as an area of study oriented toward the understanding of such spaces. That is, they noted that design was a systematic activity composed of a series of choices or design solutions which correspond to a set of possible locations in a design space (Linder & Peters, 1991).

Since then, a major area with which contemporary policy researchers have been concerned is better understanding and demarking the nature of more effective design spaces – that is, those which allow deliberations and debates to occur which lead to superior designs rather than poorer or nonexistent ones (Howlett, 2011).

These spaces are delimited and characterized by on-the-ground political realities which shape overall public and elite preferences for certain kinds of tools and mixes over others, such as market-based portfolios over state-based ones. Policy design processes, for example, are embedded within, and their effectiveness is delimited by prevailing modes and styles of governance. As an example, Ansell and Gash (2008, p. 543) underscored the significance of several "spatial" variables that are critical for the effectiveness of collaborative governance, including reconciling with "prior history of conflict or cooperation, the incentives for stakeholders to participate, power and resource imbalances, leadership and institutional design."

Table 1 Design Spaces and Expected Policy-Formulation
Processes

		Government's Ability to Alter the Status Quo	
		High	**Low**
Government's Intention to Design	High	Optimal Design Space Design via packaging	Incremental Design Space Design via patching
	Low	Stretching or Muddling Through Nondesign Space Formulation via incremental adaptation or stretching	Static Nondesign Space Garbage can–type processes

Thinking about design effectiveness, in this sense, begins with an understanding of how the policy design space influences what kinds of policies are envisioned and how such envisioning takes place. Table 1 presents a schematic illustrating a contemporary understanding of such spaces, which are affected by the presence of significant policy legacies and unique political conditions that can affect whether or not policy changes follow a design-oriented pattern of analysis and deliberation or some other form, and whether design is likely to occur by whole measures ("packaging") or in parts ("patching") (Howlett & Rayner, 2013; Howlett & Mukherjee, 2014).

As Table 1 shows, in any specific design circumstance whether or not "design" takes place at all can be seen to depend on the political aims and intention of government to undertake systemic thinking on a subject (Anderson, 1975). But even having an intention to be formal and analytical in designing and evaluating policy alternatives is not enough in itself to promote a design-centered process, since this also depends on the government's ability or capacity to undertake such an analysis and to alter the status quo. In many circumstances, even when an intention for design is present, capacity difficulties associated with a design situation result in the creation of alternatives which "patch" rather than "package" tools together in coherent and consistent ways.

Determining exactly what capacities are required in order to develop the design spaces needed to carry out complex design processes is thus a subject of much interest in the field today (Considine, 2012). In order to address these issues, policymakers and formulators need to be cognizant about the internal mechanisms of their polity and constituent policy sectors which can boost or undermine their intention to systematically develop effective policies or simply, for example, adopt expedient or politically marketable ones (Braathen & Croci, 2005; Braathen, 2007; Grant, 2010; Skodvin et al., 2010).

While work on intentionality remains rudimentary, however, recent work on policy capacity has outlined the fundamental nature of the skills and resources governments need to effectively formulate and implement policy (Bullock et al., 2001; Wu et al., 2010; Rotberg, 2014; Howlett & Ramesh, 2015, 2016). These exist at three levels: individual, organizational, and systemic (Wu et al., 2015).

Individually, those striving for effective design need to possess technical expertise for substantive policy analysis and communication of knowledge, while necessary skills of those in management roles also include leadership and negotiation expertise. Individual political acumen for understanding the interests of various stakeholders and gauging political feasibility is also a fundamental capacity for successful governance. At the *organizational* level, information mobilization capacities to facilitate policy analysis, administrative resources for successful coordination between policymaking agencies, and political support all contribute toward overall policy capacity. At the *system* level, institutions and opportunities for knowledge creation and use need to exist alongside arrangements for accountability and securing political legitimacy.

In general, governments need high levels of capability and competence in all aspects of capacity in order to effectively design policies. While shortcomings in one or a few of the dimensions may be offset by strengths along other dimensions, no government can expect to be (fully) capable if it is lacking capacity across many dimensions (Tiernan & Wanna, 2006).

Shortfalls in specific kinds of capacity are especially critical in specific modes of governance and constitute their Achilles' heel (Menahem & Stein, 2013; Howlett & Ramesh 2016) when it comes to effectively creating policy solutions for different policy problems. Hence, in recent years in many jurisdictions the default reform often adopted in practice by governments seeking to improve upon hierarchical governance has been to turn to a market or network mode of governance (Weimer & Vining, 2011). But in order to function effectively, markets require tough but sensible regulations that are diligently implemented. Having the technical knowledge to craft such regulations is thus a critical competence required for effective market-based governance. Analytical skills at the level of individual analysts and policy workers are key in this area, and the "policy analytical capacity" of government needs to be especially high in order to deal with complex quantitative economic and financial issues involved in regulating and steering the sector and preventing crises (Rayner et al., 2013).

Similarly design within legal systems of governance requires a high level of managerial skills in order to avoid diminishing returns with compliance or growing noncompliance with government rules and regulations (May, 2005). And system level capabilities are especially crucial in this mode of governance because governments will find it difficult to command and control in the absence of the target population's trust. And while network governance may perform well when dealing with design for sensitive issues such as parental supervision or elderly care (Pestoff et al., 2012), in other instances civil society and social capital may not be constructed or resourced sufficiently to be able to create beneficial network forms of governance (Tunzelmann, 2010). Networks, for example, will fail when governments encounter at the organizational level capability problems, such as a lack of societal leadership, poor associational structures, and weak state steering capacities which make adoption of network governance modes problematic (Keast et al., 2006; Klijn & Koppenjan, 2012).

3.1.2   Effective Instrument Mixes

A greater emphasis on tool mixes and on the processes that effectively create complex policy tool bundles has been a second feature of research into policy effectiveness over the last decade (Hood, 2007; Howlett, 2011). These studies have increased awareness of the many dilemmas that can appear in the path of effective policy tool or "toolkit" designs and realities (Peters & Pierre, 1998; Doremus, 2003; Sterner, 2003; Klijn & Koppenjan, 2012).

Such mixes are combinations of policy instruments that are expected to achieve particular policy objectives and which are generally seen as more efficient and effective than single instrument uses (Gunningham et al., 1998; Rogge & Reichardt, 2016). Some instruments may work well with others by nature – as is the case with "self-regulation" set within regulatory compliance frameworks (Trebilcock et al., 1979; Grabosky, 1994; Gibson, 1999) – while other combinations may not, such as, notably, independently developed subsidies and regulations. Some mixes may have evolved in a certain way which has undermined, or improved, their effectiveness, while others may have never been very effective in the first place and remain ineffective.

The new design orientation has engaged in a lengthy discussion as to how to effectively integrate policy mixes so that multiple instruments are arranged together in complex portfolios of policy goals and means (Gunningham et al., 1998; Doremus, 2003; Briassoulis, 2005; Howlett, 2011; Yi & Feiock, 2012; Peters et al., 2005; Jordan et al., 2011, 2012), often with a multilevel governance component (del Rio & Howlett, 2013). Effectively optimizing the choice of instruments in such mixes requires an additional level of knowledge of instrument-goal interactions and considerations of how mixes evolve over the long run, as well as an understanding of both long- and short-term processes of policy change. For example, a major concern of those working in the new orientation of policy design studies is whether combinations of different policy instruments, which have evolved independently and incrementally, can accomplish complex policy goals as effectively as more deliberately customized portfolios (Howlett, 2014b).

The components of such mixes include policy goals and policy means at various levels of generality (Cashore & Howlett, 2007; Howlett, 2009; Kern & Howlett, 2009), and design and instrument selection in these contexts "are all about constrained efforts to match goals and expectations both within and across categories of policy elements" (Howlett, 2009, p. 74). The various elements of policies which are combined in the design process include those related to general goals and means, those linked to tools, and those linked to the settings or calibrations of those tools (see Table 2).

Achieving effectiveness with respect to deploying such policy portfolios relies upon ensuring mechanisms, calibrations, objectives, and settings display "coherence," "consistency," and "congruence" with each other (Howlett & Rayner, 2013). Works on "smart regulation" by Neil Gunningham, Peter Grabosky, and Darren Sinclair (1998), for example, have led scholars to focus on how instruments within a policy mix or "portfolio" could effectively complement each other or conversely, lead to conflicts, resulting in guidelines for the formulation of more sophisticated policy designs in which complementarities were maximized and conflicts were avoided (Blonz et al., 2008; Barnett & Shore, 2009; Buckman & Diesendorf, 2010; Roch et al., 2010; del Rio et al., 2011).

Concerns regarding how to make the most of policy synergies while curtailing contradictions in the formulation of new policy packages are a major topic of investigation within the new design orientation (Hou & Brewer, 2010; Kiss et al., 2013; Lecuyer & Quirion, 2013). Evidence from the world concerning renewable energy and energy efficiency policy, due to climate change mitigation and energy security concerns, has revealed, for example, that

Table 2 Elements of a Policy

Policy Content	Policy Level		
	High-Level Abstraction (Policy-Level)	Operationalization (Program-Level)	On-the-Ground Specification (Measures-Level)
Policy Ends or Aims	POLICY GOALS What general types of ideas govern policy development?	PROGRAM OBJECTIVES What does policy formally aim to address?	OPERATIONAL SETTINGS What are the specific on-the-ground requirements of policy?
	(e.g., environmental protection, economic development)	(e.g., saving wilderness or species habitat, increasing harvesting levels to create processing jobs)	(e.g., considerations about sustainable levels of harvesting)
Policy Means or Tools	INSTRUMENT LOGIC What general norms guide implementation preferences?	PROGRAM MECHANISMS What specific types of instruments are utilized?	TOOL CALIBRATIONS What are the specific ways in which the instrument is used?
	(e.g., preferences for the use of coercive instruments, or moral suasion)	(e.g., the use of different tools such as tax incentives, or public enterprises)	(e.g., designations of higher levels of subsidies, the use of mandatory vs. voluntary regulatory guidelines or standards)

policy packages combining voluntary compliance with command-and-control regulation can be inherently inconsistent, bringing out contradictory responses from targets of these policy combinations (Boonekamp, 2006; del Rio et al., 2011).

Scholars of the new orientation who are concerned with design effectiveness have also been interested in how "unintended" policy mixes, created and limited by historical legacies, can be hampered due to internal inconsistencies, whereas other policy instrument groupings can be more successful in creating an internally suppor-tive combination (Grabosky, 1994; Gunningham et al., 1998; Howlett & Rayner, 2007; del Rio, 2010).

Studying complex design processes is thus concerned not only with gaining a better understanding of design "spaces" but also the temporal processes through which these spaces evolve. While some studies suggest that effective design could only occur in spaces where policy packages could be designed "en bloc" and "de novo," as already described, more recent research recognizes that most design circumstances involve building upon the foundations created in another era, often by others, and working with suboptimal design spaces. New policy design scholars are thus interested in processes such as how policy formulators, like software designers, can issue "patches" in order to correct flaws in existing mixes or allow them to adapt to changing circumstances and become more effective (Howlett, 2013; Howlett & Rayner, 2013; Rayner et al., 2013).[10]

In general, policy formulation is seen to take place while con-tained within present governance structures and the existing policy logic – restricting the number of alternatives that can be deemed feasible in such a context and decreasing the universe of policy alternatives to a smaller set of workable possibilities (Christensen et al., 2002; Meuleman, 2009a, 2009b). The "elbow room" or "degrees of freedom" designers have to maneuver in given policy

[10] In this context, the new design orientation is also interested in subjects such as policy experiments that can help to examine the possibilities of redesign (Hoffman, 2011) and in how building in temporal properties in tool mixes – adaptive policymaking (Swanson et al., 2010) – can make them more flexible or resistant to shifting conditions (Walker et al., 2010; Haasnoot et al., 2013).

design contexts is thus a subject of much interest. Many studies draw on the work of historical and sociological institutionalists such as Kathleen Thelen and colleagues (2003, 2004), who noted how macro-institutional arrangements have normally been less the product of calculated planning and more the result of processes of incremental modifications or reformulations such as "layering" or "drift" (Beland, 2007).

Contemporary research also asks questions regarding how some policy mixes may be comprised of redundant elements while others, despite containing repetitive elements, may in fact promote resiliency and adaptability (Braathen & Croci, 2005; Braathen, 2007; Swanson et al., 2010; Walker et al., 2010). In their discussion of policy element duplication, Yilin Hou and Gene Brewer (2010) have noted that the real issue is not to simply eliminate all duplication on a priori grounds but rather to design policy toolkits containing tools that work together or complement each other while being effective, given stated goals and policy contexts (Swanson et al., 2010; Hoffman, 2011).

3.1.3   The Effectiveness of Specific Policy Tools

While the discussion of effective design environments and instrument mixes have developed in parallel over the last two decades, the literature consolidating lessons regarding the specifics of effective individual tool design has also been updated to become the third leg in this stool.

Classic works on policy instrument choice, such as those by Lester Salamon, Christopher Hood, Guy Peters, and others, laid the initial groundwork toward this goal in the early 1980s. At that time scholars and practitioners focused on more precisely categorizing policy instruments and better analyzing the reasons for their use (Salamon, 1981). Careful examination of instruments and instrument choices was expected to allow practitioners to more readily draw lessons from the experiences of others with the use of particular techniques in specific circumstances, leading to more effective designs (Linder & Peters, 1984; Woodside, 1986; Bobrow & Dryzek, 1987; Dryzek & Ripley, 1988).

The key information instrument studies needed to generate in order to help facilitate better or more effective policy designs was defined from these questions (Salamon, 1981; Timmermans et al., 1998; Hood, 2007):

- What tools does a government have?
- How can these be classified?
- How have these been chosen in the past?
- Is there a pattern for this use?
- How can we explain these patterns?
- How can we improve on past patterns of use?

"Substantive" policy instruments are expected to alter some aspect of the production, distribution, and delivery of goods and services in society: broadly conceived to include both mundane goods and services such as school lunches to crude vices such as gambling or illicit drug use, to more common individual virtues such as charitable giving or volunteer work with the physically challenged, and include the attainment of collective goals like peace and security, sustainability, happiness, and well-being. They are those policy techniques or mechanisms designed to directly or indirectly affect the behavior of those involved in the production, consumption, and distribution of different kinds of goods and services in society.

This is a large field of action since it extends not only to goods and services provided or affected by markets, but also well beyond to state or public provision and regulation, as well as to those goods and services typically provided by the family, community, nonprofit, and voluntary means often with neither a firm market nor state basis (Salamon 1989; 2002).

Substantive implementation instruments can affect many aspects of production, distribution, and consumption of goods and services regardless of their institutional basis. Production effects, for example, include determining or influencing:

1 Who produces it – for example, via licensing, bureaucracy/procurement, or subsidies for new startups.

2 The types of goods and services produced – for example, through bans or limits or encouragement.

3 The quantity of goods or services provided – for example, via subsidies or quotas.

4 The quality of goods or services produced – for example, via product standards, warranties.

5 Methods of production – for example, via environmental standards or subsidies for modernization.

6 Conditions of production – for example, via health and safety standards, employment standards acts, minimum wage laws, inspections.

7 The organization of production – for example, via unionization rules, antitrust or anticombines legislation, securities legislation, or tax laws.

Consumption and distribution effects are also manifold. Some examples of these are:

1 Prices of goods and services – such as regulated taxi fares or wartime rationing.

2 Actual distribution of produced goods and services – affecting the location and types of schools or hospitals, forest tenures, or leases.

3 Level of consumer demand for specific goods – for example, through information release, nutritional and dangerous goods labeling (cigarettes), export and import taxes and bans, and similar activities.

4 Level of consumer demand in general – via interest rate, monetary and fiscal policy.

"Procedurally" oriented implementation tools, on the other hand, affect production, consumption, and distribution processes only indirectly, if at all. Instead they affect the behavior of actors involved in policy implementation. Policy actors are arrayed in various kinds of policy communities, and just as they can alter or affect the actions of citizens in the productive realm, so too can they affect and alter aspects of policymaking behavior. Procedural implementation tools are an important part of government activities aimed at altering policy interaction within policy subsystems but, as Erik-Hans Klijn et al. (1995, p. 441) put it, they "structure . . . the game without determining its outcome." That is, they affect the manner in which implementation unfolds but without predetermining the results of substantive implementation activities.

Some of the kinds of implementation-related activities that can be affected by the use of procedural tools (Klijn et al., 1995; Goldsmith & Eggers, 2004; Klijn & Koppenjan, 2006) include:

1　Changing actor policy positions
2　Setting down, defining, or refining actor positions
3　Adding actors to policy networks
4　Changing access rules for actors to governments and networks
5　Influencing network formation
6　Promoting network self-regulation
7　Modifying system-level policy parameters (e.g., levels of market reliance)
8　Changing evaluative criteria for assessing policy outcomes, success, and failure
9　Influencing the pay-off structure for policy actors
10　Influencing professional and other codes of conduct affecting policy actor behavior
11　Regulating inter-actor policy conflict
12　Changing policy actors' interaction procedures
13　Certifying or sanctioning certain types of policy-relevant behavior
14　Changing supervisory relations between actors.

Procedural implementation tools and their effects are not as well studied or understood as are substantive instruments, although several procedural techniques, such as the use of specialized investigatory commissions and government reorganizations, are quite old and well used and have been the objects of study in fields such as public administration, public management, and organizational behavior (Schneider & Sidney 2009; Lang, 2016). Nevertheless, just like their substantive counterparts, they are a key part of policy designs and policy design activity, and deriving lessons and best practices about their deployment and use remains a key element of contemporary policy design studies (Hood, 1983; Fung, 2003; Redstrom, 2006; Weaver, 2009a).

4   Moving beyond the Domestic Level: Designing Effective Global Public Policies

Although a great deal of attention has been paid to these three elements of policy design in recent years, some fundamental aspects of the design process and outcomes of that process remain poorly understood. Scholars and practitioners, for example, para-doxically now have a better sense of policy processes and process implications for design than for the designs themselves as research into the impact of policy environments and temporal legacies on policy design have led to a clearer understanding of the context and constraints under which policy formulators labor and how these affect the effectiveness of the designs which emerge through these processes, including the impact on policy mixes and bundles of tools.

However, all of this work has been done at the domestic level, and a very large outstanding question is whether the lessons from state-level studies about effectiveness applies beyond the domestic to the international level. In a world where policy developments are increasingly taking place above the nation-state level (e.g., interna-tional organization policies, regional policies, transnational policy mechanisms), it is essential that policy and administrative sciences consider not only how globalization impacts policymaking and administration domestically (Raadschelders et al., 2014), but also how their core approaches are applicable to examining the *transna-tional* (Coen & Pegram, 2015; Stone & Ladi, 2015; Moloney & Stone, 2018).

Although, as previously set out, there is a great discussion and long tradition of defining and measuring effectiveness in public policy research, as well as public management (e.g., the value approach of policy design from Mintrom & Luetjens,

2017), not all aspects of these insights can be immediately applied to transnational developments. This is because policies addressing the public are sometimes developed rather differently at the transnational level than at the national level, meaning design processes and spaces are different and often involve very different types of policy actors with different kinds of resources, capacities, and intentions.

In general, the conditions of effectiveness of policies at the transnational level are less well understood than at the domestic level. This extends to the mechanisms which give them effect as well as the "affordances" they generate for policymakers. Although early work on this subject led to some useful taxonomies and typologies of policy tools, conceptually it has not progressed much over the past twenty-five years (Chou & Ravinet, 2018).

Developing such a design agenda for "global public policies" is not purely an empirical undertaking, however. It also requires adjustments to the current conceptual toolkit of the policy design approach, which is anchored – as so many approaches within policy and administrative sciences are – in the national domain, with the "domestic" as the primary source of analytical and empirical reference. An adjusted policy design approach has strong potential for analyzing beyond-the-state policy developments. Specifically, the policy design approach is attentive to the technical dimension of policy, emphasizes the role of knowledge and expertise in design, and embraces the impact that time and sequencing has on policymaking and implementation (further elaborated in Section 4.1). These are valuable contributions that are currently scattered between social scientific fields engaged with describing and explaining international developments.

4.1 What the Policy Design Approach Offers to the Study of the Transnational Dimension

A key contribution from the policy design approach for investigating global public policy and transnational administration is its *attention to technicalities*. A design orientation embraces the technical dimension and takes seriously the assumption that technical issues have great impacts on states and citizens when implemented. Studies of interstate relations have a tendency to emphasize the macro perspective and the centrality of big states and sweeping movements has often come at the expense of excluding detailed analyses on smaller technical decisions that ultimately have great effects when implemented.

Technical issues are important in more than one way. For instance, setting spending on research at 4 percent of gross domestic product versus 2 percent may be the difference between being an innovation leader and a laggard in the market. Similarly, participating in a credit transfer scheme – in emissions trading or student mobility – means accepting how units of exchange (e.g., percentage of pollutants or number of study hours) are calculated. Disagreements may imply exclusion from the arrangement, and nonparticipation may diminish the overall attractiveness for potential investors.

In terms of beyond-the-state policy cooperation, it is often overlooked that a global "policy" may indeed consist only of technical issues that have little resemblance to the grand declaratory statements announced after worldwide summits. While it is now commonly accepted that this division between high and low politics is at best an analytical distinction with less empirical traction in the twenty-first century, policy scientists, more generally, and design scholars, more specifically, remain more attentive to the nature of policies than do scholars of international relations and politics. Indeed, policy scientists understand, and have often acknowledged in their works, the cross-cutting features of policies that amplify the impact of technical decisions. The ability to unpack how a technical decision in one policy sector affects developments across related areas is thus one benefit that the design orientation offers to studies of global public initiatives.

Another contribution of the policy design approach for studies of the transnational dimension is its *optimism concerning the roles of knowledge, expertise, and learning* in improving policy formulation and implementation. The rise of "epistocracy" or expert rule as a dominant form of governing and policymaking in some polities, such as the European Union, has generated tremendous interest and criticisms from social scientists (cf. Estlund, 2003; Dunlop, 2010; Boswell, 2012), and the design orientation adopts a unique position in these debates. This is because it assumes that scientific evidence, pragmatic know-how, and expertise, when derived suitably, should be used in matching ends (desired goals) with means (implementation tools) as a way to offer better deliveries of public services and goods (see earlier discussions on effectiveness of instrument mixes and policy tools).

This vantage point projects a certain confidence about the nature of policy that is often missing in many political and policy analyses at the domestic level, but also the international, where pessimistic accounts of national interest-driven policies and decisions often prevails. Design scholars embrace the notion that good design exists and policy problems of various magnitudes, including wicked problems and their claim of nonlinearity, can be solved, and thus promote the systematic analyses of potential solutions. This singular feature of the design orientation adds value to the study of global public policy and transnational administration by highlighting an underemphasized aspect of beyond-the-state cooperation: this interaction is often more about identifying collective problems, exchanging information, ideas, and best practices, as well as developing a common approach to these questions, than it is about (instrumental) bargaining, or what design scholars consider "nondesign."

This observation reflects the interactive and collaborative dimension of transnational governance, which not only brings together public leaders, but also societal actors. Students of beyond-the-state policy cooperation would point out that interactions at the transnational level (including intergovernmental bargaining) are often about learning, especially in repetitive interactions (i.e., iterations, where reciprocity may be a significant mechanism). In many ways, this maturation of transnational cooperation signals that the time is ripe for a design analysis of global initiatives.

The third contribution the policy design approach offers to examine global public policy and transnational administration is *its emphasis on sequencing and time.* Design scholars are attentive to sequences in policymaking and believe that the right package of "steps" can lead the way to the desired outcomes. This orientation is informed by design scholars' differentiation of implementation tools as either substantive or procedural, which is further reflected in the conceptualization of policy design as noun and verb.

Analyzing transnational developments from a policy design perspective also means taking seriously the steps in which policy formulation, instrument selection, and their implementation unfold over time. In methodological terms, to apply the design approach is to empirically map what occurs in practice sequentially. With an emphasis on sequences, policy design scholars draw attention to effects over time and how policymakers select instruments to "patch," which may be stretched beyond their intended purposes to provoke further patching in the future (Howlett & Rayner, 2013).

Such an approach is extremely useful and provides a more precise and historically informed account of global and transnational policy developments, which are often presented as a series of fluid and straightforward events that somehow fail to achieve the anticipated objectives, or lead to subtle and unexpected changes over time that amount to transformation. Many comparativists in the social sciences share this interest with time and have sought to conceptualize and theorize the mechanisms through which institutions and regimes evolve, change, or transform (cf. Pierson, 2004; Thelen, 2004; Mahoney, 2012). By highlighting the importance of sequencing, design scholars therefore underline how ideas, interests, institutions, and instruments may interact in diverse ways over time to generate the outcomes observed, something that is equally valuable at the international level.

4.2 What Does Effectiveness Mean at the Beyond-the-State Level?

Parsing out which tenets of the design orientation could contribute to studies of the transnational nevertheless raises questions concerning how and why this general disengagement between the disciplines could have occurred. Some insights can be found in how policy design scholars perceive and conceptualize the globalization phenomenon. In describing the genealogy of the policy design approach, Michael Howlett and Raul Lejano (2012) depicted policy design and globalization studies as distinct and competing fields of research. The decline of the design orientation in the late 1990s is thus explained by the rise and growing popularity of two related fields of study – governance and globalization – and revolves around the hollowing out of the state (Howlett & Lejano, 2012).

Their argument in defense of the design orientation is that the demise of the state is largely exaggerated. In this view, the state both possesses the abilities to resist globalization forces and to exercise the capacities to do so. According to Howlett and Lejano (2012), the state-centered policy design model is still relevant today. However, it is also possible to approach the debates on governance, globalization, and hollowing out of the state differently. Rather than seeing the state as being either more or less hollowed out, the emergence and evolution of transnational public and "quasi-public" policy and administration can also be perceived as manifestations of state transformation.

Adopting this position opens the door for exchange, and a starting point is to consider which further aspects of the design orientation should be adjusted, which is elaborated upon in the next section. The goal of this section is to unpack what constitutes effectiveness when discussing designing global public policy. Three preliminary clarifications of effectiveness in the policy design approach, and definition of this perspective vis-à-vis these three points, are offered; these steps enable the specification of the reasons as to why effectiveness may mean something different in the case of designing global policies.

4.2.1 Three Clarifications on Effective Policy Design

The first clarification relates to the status of the "effective design" question itself. As previously discussed, the notion of "effective policy design" is and has been omnipresent in the design and public management literatures – even when not explicitly stated. That is, as the tale of design thinking presented at the outset has shown, the goal of design is effectiveness. This is why policy-makers, implicitly or explicitly, engage in design in the first instance. As one of several analytical frameworks within policy sciences, the design orientation shares its foundational assumption that governments wish to have their goals effectively achieved in an efficient way.

As also previously discussed, however, it is not always clear to what "effectiveness" exactly refers. Is "effectiveness of policy design" a research question? Thus, does "effective policy design" become a research object that is constructed and analyzed (and eventually contested) by researchers? Or is "effective policy design" an objective for design scholars and a constitutive feature of the policy design approach's ontology? That is, do policy design scholars and practitioners explicitly seek to define the conditions for effective policy design?

These two perspectives are interweaved in the policy design approach. As Michael Howlett and Ishani Mukherjee (2014, p. 62) put it, "The fervent wish of proponents of design orientation is generally to reduce instances of poor and non-design to as few as possible … This, is expected to result in policies more likely to resolve pressing problems, correct social ills and better serve the public good."

It is thus necessary for the analysis of the international level to disentangle questions concerning design, effectiveness, and trans-national public policy that have different ontological starting points. For instance, what does effectiveness mean in a policy world transformed by globalization? How can we define or identify effective design of transnational policies? Explicitly distinguishing these issues does not eschew the possibility that effectiveness may be the ultimate outcome for design scholars and practitioners interested in designing. Indeed, research findings can be policy relevant, but it is important to think about the existence of more than one approach in the search for effectiveness. Considerations of effectiveness can actually nourish a more policy-oriented debate on global policies, not by directly recommending how to design effective global public policies, but by providing insights on the meaning of effectiveness that might be of interest to policymakers.

A second clarification essential to pushing this perspective concerns the very understanding of the words "effective" and "effectiveness." As already reviewed at the outset, an established literature in public policy and public management deals with these notions directly and indirectly. Evaluation of (effectiveness of) public policy is a significant topic of interest in public policy (Bovens et al., 2008), and has also become a very important field of study, with its own journals (*American Journal of Evaluation; Evaluation: The International Journal of Theory, Research and Practice; Evaluation: Theory and Praxis; New Directions for Evaluation*; etc.), scholarly networks, and methodological debates about how best to assess the effectiveness of policies. The perspective presented in this Element is different: the notion of effectiveness is unpacked to analyze what is at stake when actors are dealing with "effectiveness" when designing policy arrangements at the transnational level, and to show what it reveals about the transformations of policymaking in a globalizing world. In other words, this perspective is firmly anchored in a political science qualitative perspective, distinct from a policy evaluation viewpoint or a public management approach (see O'Toole, 2014, on theory of context and how globalization context may affect the management-performance linkage).

In the common language, there are two definitions of "effective" and "effectiveness." First, "effective" refers to successfully producing a desired or intended result; effectiveness is thus about success (outcome) and the ability to be successful (means). Evaluation approaches generally understand "effective" and "effectiveness" in this way, and therefore work at defining relevant templates and indicators to assess the production (and how much) of the intended results. But a second definition of "effective" is less about success and intended results than about the actual effects. "Effective" hence means operative, existing in fact, or producing an effect. Effectiveness in this second perspective would be about "operativeness," or acknowledgment of the production of an effect.

In policy design studies, it can be observed that the understanding of effectiveness generally corresponds to the first one and that there is a tendency to neglect or elude the second perspective. In this way, focusing on the overall search for the effective design and specific "intended results," the risk may be to miss all the other effects the policy instruments may trigger. The initial or observable effects may ultimately lead to the very effectiveness the designers seek, albeit through other combinations of effect or with the lapse of time (e.g., some instruments require a longer duration to take effect). Some effects may not be anticipated (this corresponds to the well-known category of unintended effects), but one can also imagine a specific type of policy design that leaves room for open effects. To understand the development of global policy arrangements, it is particularly important to adopt an effectiveness questioning which encompasses both meanings: effectiveness as success in producing intended results *and* effectiveness as "operativeness" and production of effects that are to be characterized.

A third clarification required in this discussion about design, effectiveness, and the transnational dimension deals with the "effectiveness of what" question. In policy design literature, and because of the approach's optimism vis-à-vis the improvement of public policy, there tends to be an overlap between the ideas of an effective policy *design* on the one hand and an effective *policy* on the other.

Broadly, the core idea is that when a design is "smart," governments then select the right implementation tools, consisting of substantive and procedural tools, for a rightly identified policy problem. Within this formulation, largely based on a rational choice perspective of actor behavior, any outcomes suggesting failure would simply mean that the wrong implementation tools were chosen or the "preconditions" for design were absent or unfavorable (Howlett & Mukherjee, 2014). Once the right tools are picked when the favorable conditions are present, the assumption goes, the anticipated policy results should be observed. Hence in this approach effective policy *design* should lead to *effective policy*, and conceptually it is less important to work on the distinction between effective design and effective policy, which tends to belong to a single category.

However, there is no reason to assume that there is automaticity between effective design and effective policy. Policy design scholars' argument on preconditions generally excludes the contemplation of different combination types of effectiveness between design and policy. In a world in which not all preconditions can always be foreseen, one can imagine a situation in which effective design leads to ineffective policy. While one may attribute this to bounded rationality, it can also be that some implementers simply refuse to execute the agreed upon and adopted policy for reasons that may not be political or rational.

A situation in which ineffective design ends up with an effective policy is equally conceivable. For example, in instances in which design is poor, policy actors may still achieve the policy goal through creative interpretation, or abandonment, of the policy means. While these outcomes may be less of a concern at the domestic level, where actor participation is more easily arranged and monitored, they may be more prevalent and important at the international level. So, for the study of global public policy it is important to consider that questions concerning "effectiveness of design" and "effectiveness of policy" may be more autonomous than usually assumed by the design literature. Table 3 summarizes these three clarifications, and the next section elaborates why policy effectiveness may take on a different meaning when examining transnational initiatives.

4.2.2 The Reasons Why Effectiveness Means Something Different at the Global Level

Although the more comprehensive understanding of effective design proposed here is not meant to be particular to global policy developments, there are some specifics to the design of global policies that ensure a revisited questioning on effectiveness is particularly useful.

Table 3 Three Clarifications on Effectiveness in a Revisited
Approach to Design

	Classical Policy Design Literature	**Revisited Policy Design**
Status of effectiveness question	Research question integrated with the ambition to improve policymaking	Primarily a research question
Understanding of effectiveness	Effectiveness is a production of the intended results/ "success"	Effectiveness is a production of effects (intended or not)
Effectiveness of what?	Effectiveness of design means effective policy	Effectiveness of design and effectiveness of policy are autonomous questions

The first thing that is different about the design of global policies, which then implies a different understanding of their effectiveness, has to do with the great variety of actors involved. Applying the policy design approach to studies of global public policy and transnational administration requires *a renewed understanding of the types of actors* who may be involved in policymaking (Chou & Ravinet, 2018). In the design literature, and even with the theoretical efforts of the new design orientation to develop a more open perspective on the design space (see the preceding section), the state is often seen as the key policy actor and is operationalized as the government (central or regional) responsible for decision-making across all stages of the policy cycle, sequential or otherwise. Taking this research design to the transnational level would imply that attention is focused primarily on analyzing the behavior of governments, which offers only a limited view. As the governance approach reminds us, interactive and collaborative forms of governance require the bringing together of public leaders with societal actors, as well as individuals from the business or scientific communities. Hence, while it is possible to keep the policy design core principle to concentrate on the notion of intentionality and view design as an act of purposive actors, studying global initiatives requires broadening the range of participant actors. In the case of global and transnational policymaking, the purposive actors involved in design are generally not predetermined, they may wear multiple hats, and they may follow a sectoral organizational logic that is extremely relevant and significant.

Indeed, as Diane Stone and Stella Ladi (2015, p. 844) put it, "The constitutive actors of global processes and transnational administration may be different from the domestic level, or they may have demonstrated increased power beyond the state" – and thus their identification and relationship (if any) with the state should be elaborated through empirical research, which can only occur when the analytical perspective does not preclude this exploration. For instance, there are multiple design actors at the transnational level including, but are not limited to (1) formal or official actors (they include governments and international governmental organizations) and (2) nonstate actors and networks. International and regional organizations are involved in a variety of design activities, including, for instance, developing new programs for internal and external coordination (e.g., standards and benchmarks), for (client) countries, and for global or regional public-private partnerships and networks. Added to this grouping are the international consultancy firms (often contracted by governments and international/regional organizations to deliver design on procedural processes and evaluate implementation), think tanks, global commissions and taskforces, large international nongovernmental organizations (designers of indexes or rankings), business associations, and accreditation bodies. Although this list is not exhaustive, it does point to the many design actors at the transnational level who work with governments or on their behalf.

This has important implications for the understanding of effectiveness. In the design of global policies, not only might the number of actors involved be greater, but more fundamentally, the type of actors might be extremely diverse. This means that the possibility of convergence on the meaning of effectiveness may be much more challenging than could be feasibly conceived. Meanings are actually intersubjective, and the more diverse the actors involved, the more intersubjectivity is involved. Agreements upon ambivalent general objectives (sustainable development, for instance) or upon technical small objectives (that might be equally acceptable for different or even contradictory world visions), rather than on defined policy objective, are extremely likely in the design of global policies. In the case of ambivalence, what happens is that actors mask their real objectives and understanding; but when it comes to moments of evaluating effectiveness, ambivalence might not be manageable. In the case of small technical objectives, this might be problematic as well in terms of defining effectiveness: evaluating effectiveness is not only about looking at whether scattered small objectives were reached in isolation from one another, but also about how the combination of different indicators allows the evaluators to measure the overall policy outcome.

A second feature that is specific in designing global public policies deals with policy instruments. A design orientation to studying transnational developments should also adjust the *potential range and types of policy instruments* that actors may have at their disposal. The extant policy design literature depicts instrument selection (picking them up from a toolbox) as one of the core activities of the design process. This is a problematic formulation for transnational developments or initiatives in at least two ways. First, it assumes that instrument selection is a neutral act and reveals nothing about the relationship between the governing and the governed (Lascoumes & Le Gales, 2007). It is common knowledge in several strands of political science literature that governments use transnational policy arenas for domestic purposes, including tying their hands to supranational reforms they wished to introduce domestically but which are opposed by veto players (Guiraudon, 2000).

These supranational processes are not purely bargaining as they also involve deliberation of policy problems and matching potential solutions with outcomes. Any perception of instrument failure following these processes is thus less straightforward, and lessons to be learned are more challenging to extract. Design scholars acknowledge this possibility, but they often relegate such developments with references to complexity without adequately engaging in the unpacking of what complexity means for the design orientation. As noted already, the politics of making decisions about complex or wicked problems have yet to be fully explored.

Second, the existence of an instrument toolbox from which to "pick and choose" may be unavailable at the transnational level. This may be the result of some involved policy actors lacking the authority to invoke access to certain instruments, or it may be that transnational policy instrumentation is a process more about invention and innovation than about selecting among available tools. While more empirical observations are certainly needed to refine the analytical construct of the design orientation, existing findings already point to the general inaccuracy of categorizing these instances as preconditions for or against design.

Combined with the first specific feature of global public policies (diversity of actors involved in design), this has important implications for defining effectiveness. As noted earlier, actors might agree or disagree on the objectives, and as far as tools are concerned they might be available or unavailable. Four distinct scenarios can thus be envisioned (see Table 4). First, in a scenario in which the actors agree on the general objectives, the relevant tools available and actors entitled to use them, classical policy design assumptions may be applied; this scenario, however, is far less likely to emerge consistently at the transnational level for reasons mentioned earlier. Second, when actors disagree on the general objective in a scenario in which instruments are available, they would tend to agree on small technical instruments; this is a common scenario observed in transnational policy coordination. The third scenario sees actors disagreeing over general objectives in which there are no instruments readily available; this is another frequent scenario at the global level, where policy cooperation results in no concrete

Table 4 Actor Agreement and Instrument Availability

		Availability of Instruments	
		Yes	*No*
Actor Agreement on General Objective	*Agree*	• Classical policy design assumption • Less likely at the global level	• Tools do not exist; actors have to innovate • Tools exist but actors are not authorized to use them
	Disagree	Agreement on small technical objectives/tools	No public policy output (but does not mean there are no effects at all)

Note: the two dimensions of agreement and instrument availability can evolve over time.

steps forward. Finally, the fourth scenario reveals actors agreeing on the general objective, but the tools do not exist (i.e., actors need to innovate) or the actors lack the authority to use existing tools.

The third specificity in the design of global public policies that has implications for the definition of effectiveness deals with the "line of command." Any policy design incorporates an implementation template of not only which instruments will be used, but also of the different policy and administrative bodies that will be involved at different policy levels within this process. This is what can be designated as the notion of the "line of command." What is specific in the design of global public policies is actually that the number of layers, and therefore intermediary policy bodies or delegated actors involved between the global objective and the final implementation on the policy ground, might be many. Indeed, the "line of command" between designing and implementing global policies is longer, more complex, and potentially filled with ambiguity in comparison to those associated with domestic policies where the "line of

Table 5 Specific Features of Global Policies and Implications for Defining Effectiveness

	Specificities in Designing Global Policies	What They Imply about Effectiveness
About Types of Actors	Great variety of actors, varying relationship with the state	Highly inter-subjective meanings when evaluating effectiveness
About Instruments	There is no "ready-made" toolbox at hand; tools are not neutral	Discourse on effectiveness is challenging to have in advance
About the Line of Command	Longer and more complex line of command	Effectiveness of design as an end itself rather than an outcome (an effect)

command" is comparatively shorter, clearer, and deeply institutionalized with taken-for-granted assumptions concerning actor behavior.

This specificity of global public policies from the vantage point of the "line of command" has implications for the definition of effectiveness. The universe of final implementation is likely to be very far from the one of the initial design (in space and time), and the initial design thinking may thus be very diffused or nonexistent among actors tasked with policy implementation. This results in a different understanding of the "effectiveness of what" question that has already been mentioned. Given the distance between policy design and final implementation, actors tasked with evaluation are far more likely to privilege an understanding of effectiveness to the *design* rather than what actually emerges (policy outcomes) on the ground. When final implementation is far and uncertain, appreciating design effectiveness is obviously a more conceivable, feasible, and satisfying approach than appreciating the final effects of implementing the policy. Table 5 summarizes the specific features of global policies from the perspectives of the types of actors, instruments, and line of command, as well as their implications for defining (and ultimately assessing) effectiveness at the transnational level.

4.3 Adding Conceptual Tools to the Policy Design Toolbox: Framing and Embracing an Inductive Approach to Effectiveness

Opening up the policy design approach to studying beyond-the-state-level developments invites discussions concerning which analytical and methodological tools could be useful in this undertaking. This section elaborates one such tool: framing and frames. This discussion is not meant to be exclusive; rather, it is an extension of an invitation to consider how to advance the debate about policy design, effectiveness, and the transnational dimension.

The literature on framing is large and spans across multiple fields: from psychology, linguistics, discourse analysis, sociology, political science, to public policy and European Union studies (Mazey & Richardson, 1997; Harcourt, 1998; Dudley & Richardson, 1999; Morth, 2000; Geddes & Guiraudon, 2004; Daviter, 2007). In the most general sense, the framing approach emphasizes the importance of framing dynamics in accounting for the final contours of policies, politics, and polities. A classic definition of framing is "a way of selecting, organizing, interpreting, and making sense of a complex reality so as to provide guideposts for knowing, analyzing, persuading, and adapting" (Rein & Schön, 1991, p. 263). By examining this selection process, the constitutive elements of designing and how they move toward effectiveness can be identified.

Like designing, framing does not take place in a political vacuum. Here, venue selection is important because it generally delimits which actors (officials from international organizations, public leaders, societal representatives, scientists and scholars, or lobbyists for business) have access and have the authority to determine which other actors are allowed to participate. This is an important distinction, especially for the beyond-the-state developments and the current discussion of what constitutes "effectiveness" in policy design. Frank Baumgartner and Bryan Jones (1991), for instance, explain how beliefs and values concerning a particular policy (the "policy image") interact with the existing set of political institutions (i.e., the venue of action). "Each venue," they argue, "carries with it a decisional bias" because "the image of a policy and its venue are closely related" (Baumgartner & Jones 1991, p. 1047; see Daviter, 2007, and Guiraudon, 2000, for more granular accounts of "policy image," venue selection, and bias). For global public policies, with its multiple actors (state, semistate, and nonstate actors), this insight from framing points to the difficulty of stating clearly a priori what effectiveness means for each of the actors, and what an effective public policy at the global level would look like as it may evolve throughout the policy cycle toward implementation.

Framing thus refers to a selection process in which policy actors understand, present, debate, justify, or contest aspects of an issue (e.g., venue selection, problem identification) following an overriding evaluative criterion known as "frames" (more on frames in the following paragraphs). Although most studies using the framing approach focus on the agenda-setting stage, framing has been approached as a more dynamic and sequential process (see Harcourt, 1998; Geddes & Guiraudon, 2004; Cerna & Chou, 2014). Indeed, framing and reframing has been conceptualized (Cerna & Chou, 2014) as a process through which public policy outcomes (including effectiveness) can be explained. Thus, conceptualizing policy design as a process of continuous framing and reframing would be to take each sequence of the policy process seriously as a standalone case for analysis, albeit with the knowledge of its appearance in the entire sequence and thus its relationship with the sequence before and after. This approach is far more likely to capture the various effects of public policy that may or may not appear to be successful as previously elaborated.

Frames are therefore integral to an approach based on framing, but the constitutive parts of frames are not often specified even though the notion of frames is frequently used. Robert

Entman (1993, p. 52) argues that frames perform four distinct functions: define problems, diagnose causes, make moral judgments, and suggest remedies. Whereas frames are more commonly associated with the earlier stages of the policy cycle, frames are present at every stage of the policy cycle, including implementation and evaluation; hence frames have implications for assessing policy effectiveness. Frames can be identified through these constitutive parts: an *associated discourse* conveying actors' understanding of the task at hand (e.g., *problem definition*), their value judgment or *vision,* and their proposed ways, or the standard operating procedures, to go about tackling the policy problem or *policy solution.* This broad definition indicates that there are a great variety of frames in the framing literature, including *sectoral* frames, *political* frames, as well as *evaluation* frames. When examining the effectiveness of design at the transnational dimension, specifying the relevant frames would be at least one of the steps forward.

Adding the analytical tool of framing, along with a clear distinction of the constitutive parts of a frame, to the design conceptual toolbox encourages embracing an inductive approach to empirically unpack what effectiveness means to the various policy actors involved or excluded. In practice, this would promote a more qualitative approach, involving, for instance, interviews with the relevant policy actors (mapping the constellation of actors and their views), participant observation of their exchanges (in policy dialogues, or as part of the monitoring and evaluation team), as well as analysis of the adopted and draft position papers and reports.

These methods enable an identification of the actual range of policy frames that were active in the sequences under study. To begin probing whether or not the positions and policies adopted at those sequences are effective, it is thus essential to examine these sequences as part of a continual framing-reframing process. Here, the questions that can be raised and addressed include (1) Are the frames consistent throughout the entire framing-reframing process? (2) If not, how were the frames

replaced, revised, or challenged? (3) Do the excluded frames ree-
merge at the latter sequences, and, if so, what enabled their
appearance? Embedded in these questions is an implicit understanding that actors may change their positions over time (see
Table 4), and different actors may occupy the different sequences
(see Table 5). In short, the transnational dimension offers a new
analytical space filled with empirical possibilities to test emergent
assumptions about design and effectiveness.

5 Next Steps for Design Thinking and Effectiveness

Policy design is central to the policy process, and research and
thinking in this area have developed significantly since its incep-
tion as a concept a number of years ago. That development has
involved the study of policy instruments and attempts to better
define and understand policy problems. These intellectual developments are important in themselves but, as this Element has
demonstrated, design is perhaps most important as the means
through which the effectiveness of public policies can be
enhanced.

This Element therefore set out to explore what "effectiveness"
means when designing public policies at the state and beyond-the-
state level. Effectiveness was unpacked in several ways, including
identifying how the global layer presents a distinct challenge and
opportunity for the effectiveness research agenda with its presence
of multiple actors (state, semistate, and nonstate), an unclear set of
policy instruments at their disposal, and a broken chain of command from the global to the local in terms of implementation.
As discussed, much of the first and second waves of design have
focused on finding effective "solutions" for problems, even if in
reality very few policy problems are really solved. More contemporary approaches to design, or designing, eschew those definite
solutions in favor of more process-oriented interventions that may
only aspire for shorter-terms equilibria rather than solutions.

This tale of the development of policy design reflects to some
degree the continuing struggle between more synoptic

conceptions of policy and thinking about policy more in terms of incrementalism, bounded rationality, and search of broader legitimation. Design has generally represented an attempt to present a comprehensive and synoptic policy choice that will actually solve a problem. While that hubris about the capacity to make definitive interventions has generally been thwarted by the realities of the world, the desire to craft solutions for policy problems remains a paramount concern for policymakers. And the attempt to develop algorithms linking problems and solutions remains important to many in the academic community working on policy questions.

While the hopes of the comprehensive designers may be thwarted all too often, the incremental prescriptions for policy design persist also. Rather than creating "THE" answer for the problem, the incrementalists would hope for a "good enough" solution in the short run, one that would ameliorate the problem without actually solving it once and for all. As the design literature has evolved, this less confident perspective on policy formulation has become more prevalent. At the extreme, as has already been shown, the careful design of processes may supplant the substantive design of interventions as the model manner of thinking about policy design.

What is perhaps unfortunate in this development is the failure of the two approaches to communicate effectively. Designers tend not to think about incremental solutions, while incrementalists may not recognize that their short-term design interventions constitute de facto experiments in design. If these two sets of actors, as we see them, were engaged in more conscious thoughts about the linkages of the two forms of policy activity, there might be greater possibilities of making *designing* a more viable solution for the design question.

Similarly, there is the issue of design at different level of government than the central state, a subject which has only begun to be examined. To a certain extent the literature on policy design is, as shown already in the beginning of this Element, a rich and mature field of research. Several reviews (cf. Howlett & Lejano, 2012;

Howlett & Mukherjee, 2014) describe the theoretical and substantive contributions the design orientation has made to enrich contemporary understanding of public policymaking and implementation effects. But as this Element has demonstrated, one of the emerging needs of design thinking is to include considerations for designing policy effectiveness at the transnational level. In a world characterized by wicked and complex problems, states have sought increased cooperation with one another, seeking (or perhaps hoping) to find solutions for their challenges, and understanding how these are designed is a pressing issue in the policy design world.

This discussion highlights a further aspect of designing for effectiveness which is raised in this Element: that attention to politics in general has been insufficient in existing design studies. This is manifested in two ways. The first is that policy problems (wicked or tame) are both perceptual and objective, and outside of the path-breaking work of Schneider and Ingram, insufficient attention has been paid to the perceptual nature of the problems policymakers face. That is, policy problems simply do not arise in some objective sense, although they do have an objective component, but they must be understood as the objects of a political process. Defining the nature of a policy problem and its level of tractability is a crucial component of the political process involved in constructing policy interventions, as the extensive literature on framing and reframing (Schön & Rein, 1994; Hisschemoller & Hoppe, 1995) discussed in the preceeding section has demonstrated.

Further, the politics of making decisions about wicked problems has also not been fully articulated. While there have been some discussions in the policy design literature about making policy decisions in the presence of uncertainty and complexity (Funke, 1991; Walker et al., 2010; Room, 2011), the particular demands of making decisions in conditions of high uncertainty have been explored relatively little. These types of problems, which may be more prevalent in the early twenty-first century than in the past (Levin et al., 2012), may produce strong political reactions as their inherent difficulties become apparent and the lack of effectiveness of conventional remedies becomes equally visible (Nair & Howlett, 2017).

This discussion also opened up the possibility of adding new analytical tools to the design toolbox and proposed framing and frames as one potentially useful tool for studying effectiveness at both the domestic and global public policy levels. By conceptualizing policy design as a sequence of framing and reframing and specifying the constitutive parts of a frame, it was suggested that the exercise of "adding more analytical tools" can be very useful for the policy design agenda to further consider and engage with other literatures on the subject of effectiveness. This is true of studies of the effectiveness of overarching policy objectives, on effectiveness of project design, on effectiveness of project implementation among others, and on effectiveness and legitimation (of the problem, of the process, of the result). In short, there are many ways forward for this very exciting research agenda on designing for policy effectiveness.

References

Alexander, E. (1982). Design in the decision-making process. *Policy Sciences*, 14, 279–92.

Anderson, J. E. (1975). *Public Policymaking*, New York, NY: Praeger.

Ansell, C. & Gash, A. (2008). Collaborative governance in theory and practice. *Journal of Public Administration Research and Theory*, 18(4), 543–71.

Banfield, E. C. (1977). Policy science as metaphysical madness. In R. A. Goldwin, ed., *Statesmanship and Bureaucracy*. Washington, DC: American Enterprise Institute for Public Policy, pp. 1–35.

Barker, A. & Peter, B. G. eds. (1993). *The Politics of Expert Advice: Creating, Using and Manipulating Scientific Knowledge for Public Policy*. Pittsburgh, PA: University of Pittsburgh Press.

Barnett, C. K. & Shore, B. (2009). Reinventing program design: challenges in leading sustainable institutional change. *Leadership & Organization*, 30(1), 16–35.

Barzelay, M. (2001). *The New Public Management: Improving Research and Policy Dialogue*. Berkeley, CA: University of California Press.

Bason, C. (2014). *Design for Policy*. Burlington, VT: Gower.

Baumgartner, F. & Jones, B. (1991). Agenda dynamics and policy subsystems. *Journal of Politics*, 53(4), 1044–74.

Beland, D. (2007) Ideas and institutional change in social security: conversion, layering and policy drift. *Social Science Quarterly*, 88(1), 20–38.

Blonz, J. A., Vajjhala, S. P. & Safirova, E. (2008). *Growing complexities: a cross-sector review of US biofuels policies and their interactions*. Resources for the Future (RFF) Discussion Paper No. RFF DP 08-47. Available at www.rff.org/files/sharepoint/WorkImages/Download/RFF-DP-08-47_final.pdf (last accessed 30 September 2017).

Bobrow, D. B. (2006). Policy design: ubiquitous, necessary and difficult. In B. G. Peters & J. Pierre, eds., *Handbook of Public Policy*. Thousand Oaks, CA: Sage, pp. 75–96.

Bobrow, D. B. & Dryzek, J. S. (1987). *Policy Analysis by Design*, Pittsburgh, PA: University of Pittsburgh Press.

Boonekamp, P. G. M. (2006). Actual interaction effects between policy measures for energy efficiency: a qualitative matrix method and quantitative simulation results for households. *Energy*, 31(14), 2848–73.

Boswell, C. (2012). *The Political Uses of Expert Knowledge: Immigration Policy and Social Research*. Cambridge: Cambridge University Press.

Botterill, L. C. & Hindmoor, A. (2012). Turtles all the way down: bounded rationality in an evidence-based age. *Policy Studies*, 33, 367–79.

Bovens, M., 't Hart, P. & Kuipers, S. (2008). The politics of policy evaluation. In R. E. Goodin, M. Moran, & M. Rein, eds., *The Oxford Handbook of Public Policy*. Oxford: Oxford University Press, pp. 319–35.

Braathen, N. A. (2007). Instrument mixes for environmental policy: how many stones should be used to kill a bird? *International Review of Environmental and Resource Economics*, 1(2), 185–235.

Braathen, N. A. & Croci, E. (2005). Environmental agreements used in combination with other policy instruments. In E. Croci, ed., *The Handbook of Environmental Voluntary Agreements: Design, Implementation and Evaluation Issues*. Dordrecht: Springer, pp. 335–64.

Briassoulis, H. (2005). *Policy Integration for Complex Environmental Problems*. Aldershot: Ashgate.

Buckman, G. & Diesendorf, M. (2010). Design limitations in Australian renewable electricity policies. *Energy Policy*, 38(7), 3365–76.

Bullock, H., Mountford, J. & Stanley, R. (2001). *Better Policy-Making*. London: Centre for Management and Policy Studies, Cabinet Office, United Kingdom.

Capano, G., Howlett, M. & Ramesh, M. (forthcoming). Designing for robustness: surprise, agility and improvisation in policy design. *Policy & Society*.

Capano, G., & Woo, J. J. (2017). Resilience and robustness in policy design: a critical appraisal. *Policy Sciences*, 50(3), 399–426.

Caplan, N., & Weiss, C. H. (1977). *A Minimal Set of Conditions Necessary for the Utilization of Social Science Knowledge in Policy Formulation at the National Level*. Lexington, KY: Lexington Books.

Cashore, B. & Howlett, M. (2007). Punctuating what equilibrium? Institutional rigidities and thermostatic properties in Pacific Northwest forest policy dynamics. *American Journal of Political Science*, 51(3), 532–51.

Cerna, L. & Chou, M.-H. (2014). The regional dimension in the global competition for talent: lessons from framing the European Scientific Visa and Blue Card. *Journal of European Public Policy*, 21(1), 76–95.

Chou, M.-H. & Ravinet, P. (forthcoming). Designing global public policies in the 21st century. In K. Moloney & D. Stone, eds., *Handbook on Global Policy and Transnational Administration*. Oxford: Oxford University Press.

Christensen, T., Laegreid, P. & L. R. Wise. (2002). Transforming administrative policy. *Public Administration*, 80(1), 153–79.

Coen, D. & Pegram, T. (2015). Wanted: a third generation of global governance and research. *Governance: An International Journal of Policy, Administration and Institutions*, 28(4), 417–20.

Colebatch, H. K. (2017). The idea of policy design: intention, process, outcome, meaning and validity. *Public Policy and Administration*, publishing online: May 18, 2017. https://doi.org/10.1177/0952076717709525 (last accessed 11 December 11 2017).

Considine, M. (2012). Thinking outside the box? Applying design theory to public policy. *Politics & Policy*, 40(4), 704–24.

Considine, M., Alexander, D. & Lewis, J. M. (2009). *Networks, Innovation and Public Policy: Politicians, Bureaucrats and Pathways to Change Inside Government*. Basingstoke: Macmillan.

Considine, M., Alexander, D. & Lewis, J. M. (2014). Policy design as craft: design expertise using a semi-experimental approach. *Policy Sciences*, 47, 209–25.

Craft, J. & Howlett, M. (2012). Policy formulation, governance shifts and policy influence: location and content in policy advisory systems. *Journal of Public Policy* 32(2), 79–98.

Daviter, F. (2007). Policy framing in the European Union. *Journal of European Public Policy*, 14(4), 654–66.

de Leon, P. (1997). *Democracy and the Policy Sciences*, Albany, NY: State University of New York Press.

del Río, P. (2010). Analysing the interactions between renewable energy promotion and energy efficiency support schemes: the impact of different instruments and design elements. *Energy Policy*, 38(9), 4978–89.

del Río, P. & Howlett, M. (2013). "Beyond the 'Tinbergen Rule' in Policy Design: Matching Tools and Goals in Policy Portfolios." SSRN Scholarly Paper. Available at https://papers.ssrn.com/sol3/papers.cfm?abstract_id=2247238 (last accessed 30 September 2017).

del Río, P., Silvosa, A. C. & Gómez, G. I. (2011). Policies and design elements for the repowering of wind farms: a qualitative analysis of different options. *Energy Policy*, 39(4), 1897–1908.

Doremus, H. (2003). A policy portfolio approach to biodiversity protection on private lands. *Environmental Science & Policy*, 6, 217-32.

Dryzek, J. S. (1983). Don't toss coins into garbage cans: a prologue to policy design. *Journal of Public Policy*, 3, 345-67.

Dryzek, J. S. & Ripley, B. (1988). The ambitions of policy design. *Policy Studies Review*, 7(4), 705-19.

Dudley, G. & Richardson, J. (1999). Competing advocacy coalitions and the process of "frame reflection": a longitudinal analysis of EU steel policy. *Journal of European Public Policy*, 6(2), 225-48.

Dunlop, C. A. (2010). The temporal dimension of knowledge and the limits of policy appraisal: biofuels policy in the UK. *Policy Sciences*, 43 (4), 343-63.

Elmore, R. F. (1985). Forward and backward mapping: reversible logic in the analysis of public policy. In K. Hanf & T. A. J. Toonen, eds., *Policy Implementation in Federal and Unitary States*, Dordrecht: Martinus Nijhoff, pp. 76-98.

Entman, R. M. (1993). Framing: toward clarification of a fractured paradigm. *Journal of Communication*, 43(4), 51-8.

Estlund, D. (2003). Why not epistocracy? In N. Reshotko, ed., *Desire, Identity and Existence: Essays in Honor of T. M. Penner*. Kelowna, BC: Academic Printing and Publishing, pp.53-69.

Fung, A. (2003). Survey article: recipes for public spheres: eight institutional design choices and their consequences. *Journal of Political Philosophy*, 11(3), 338-67.

Funke, J. (1991). Solving complex problems: exploration and control of complex systems. In R. Sternberg & P. Frensch, eds., *Complex Problem Solving - Principles and Methods*. Hillsdale, NJ: Lawrence Earlbaum Association.

Geddes, A. & Guiraudon, V. (2004). Britain, France, and EU anti-discrimination policy: the emergence of an EU policy paradigm. *West European Politics*, 27(2), 334-53.

Gibson, R. B., ed. (1999). *Voluntary Initiatives: The New Politics of Corporate Greening*. Peterborough, ON: Broadview Press.

Gilabert, P. & Lawford-Smith, H. (2012). Political feasibility: a conceptual exploration. *Political Studies*, 60(4), 809-25.

Goldsmith, S. & Eggers, W. D. (2004). *Governing by Network: The New Shape of the Public Sector*. Washington, DC: Brookings Institution Press.

Grabosky, P. N. (1994). Green markets: environmental regulation by the private sector. *Law and Policy*, 16(4), 419-48.

Grant, W. (2010). Policy instruments in the Common Agricultural Policy. *West European Politics*, 33(1), 22–38.

Guiraudon, V. (2000). European integration and migration policy: vertical policy-making as venue shopping. *Journal of Common Market Studies*, 38(2), 251–71.

Gunningham, N., Grabosky, P. N. & Sinclair, D. (1998). *Smart Regulation: Designing Environmental Policy*. Oxford: Clarendon Press.

Haasnoot, M., Kwakkel, J. H., Walker, W. E. (2013). Dynamic adaptive policy pathways: a method for crafting robust decisions for a deeply uncertain world. *Global Environmental Change*, 23(2), 485–98.

Hallerberg, M. & Wehner, J. (2013). "The Technical Competence of Economic Policy-Makers in Developed Democracies." SSRN Scholarly Paper, July 29, 2013. Available at http://papers.ssrn.com/abst ract=2191490 (last accessed 15 December 15, 2017).

Halligan, J. (1995). Policy advice and the public sector. In B. G. Peters & D. T. Savoie, eds., *Governance in a Changing Environment*. Montreal, QC: McGill-Queen's University Press, pp. 138–72.

Harcourt, A. J. (1998). EU media ownership regulation: conflict over the definition of alternatives. *Journal of Common Market Studies*, 36(3), 369–89.

Hawkesworth, M. (1992). Epistemology and policy analysis. In W. Dunn & R. M. Kelly, eds., *Advances in Policy Studies*. New Brunswick, NJ: Transaction Publishers, pp. 291–329.

Hay, C. & Smith, N. J.-A. (2010). How policy-makers (really) understand globalization: the internal architecture of Anglophone globalization discourse in Europe. *Public Administration*, 88(4), 903–27.

Hayes, M. T. (2006). *Incrementalism and Public Policy*. Lanham, MD: University Press of America.

Head, B. W. (2016). Toward more "evidence-informed" policy making? *Public Administration Review*, 76(3), 472–84.

Hisschemöller, M. & Hoppe, R. (1995). Coping with intractable controversies: the case of problem structuring in policy design and analysis. *Knowledge and Policy*, 8, 40–60.

Hjern, B. & Porter, D. O. (1981). Implementation structures: a new unit of administrative analysis. *Organization Studies*, 2(3), 211–27.

Hoffman, M. J. (2011). *Climate Governance at the Crossroads: Experimenting with a Global Response for Kyoto*. Oxford: Oxford University Press.

Hood, C. (1983). Using bureaucracy sparingly. *Public Administration*, 61 (2), 197–208.

Hood, C. (2002). The risk game and the blame game. *Government and Opposition*, 37(1), 15-54.

Hood, C. (2007). Intellectual obsolescence and intellectual makeovers: reflections on the tools of government after two decades. *Governance*, 20(1), 127-44.

Hood, C. & Margetts, H. Z. (2007). *The Tools of Government in the Digital Age.* Basingstoke: Palgrave Macmillan.

Hou, Y. & Brewer, G. (2010). Substitution and supplementation between co-functional policy instruments: evidence from state budget stabilization practices. *Public Administration Review*, 70(6), 914-24.

Howlett, M. (2004). Beyond good and evil in policy implementation: instrument mixes, implementation styles and second-generation theories of policy instrument choice. *Policy and Society*, 23(2), 1-17.

Howlett, M. (2009). Governance modes, policy regimes and operational plans: a multi-level nested model of policy instrument choice and policy design. *Policy Sciences*, 42(1), 73-89.

Howlett, M. (2011). *Designing Public Policies: Principles and Instruments.* New York, NY: Routledge.

Howlett, M. (2013). Policy work, policy advisory systems and politicization. *Central European Journal of Public Policy*, 7(1), 4-7.

Howlett, M. (2014a). From the "old" to the "new" policy design: design thinking beyond markets and collaborative agreements. *Policy Sciences*, 47(3), 187-207.

Howlett, M. (2014b). Policy design: what, who, how and why? In C. Halpern, P. Lascoumes & P. Le Gales, eds., *L'instrumentation de l'action publique*. Paris: Presses de Sciences Po, pp. 281-316.

Howlett, M. & Lejano, R. P. (2012). Tales from the crypt: the rise and fall (and rebirth?) of policy design. *Administration & Society*, 45(3), 357-81.

Howlett, M. & Mukherjee, I. (2014). Policy design and non-design: towards a spectrum of policy formulation types. *Politics and Governance*, 2(2), 57-71.

Howlett, M., Mukherjee, I. & Woo, J. J. (2015). The new design orientation in policy formulation research: from tools to toolkits in policy instrument studies. *Policy and Politics*, 43(2), 291-311.

Howlett, M. & Ramesh, M. (2015). The two orders of governance failure: design mismatches and policy capacity issues in modern governance. *Policy and Society*, 33(4), 317-27.

Howlett, M. & Ramesh, M. (2016). Achilles' heels of governance: critical capacity deficits and their role in governance failures. *Regulation & Governance*, 10(4), 301-13.

Howlett, M. & Rayner, J. (2007). Design principles for policy mixes: cohesion and coherence in "new governance arrangements." *Policy and Society*, 26(4), 1–18.

Howlett, M. & Rayner, J. (2013). Patching vs. packaging in policy formulation: assessing policy portfolio design. *Politics and Governance*, 1(2), 170–82.

Howlett, M., Vince, J. & del Río, P. (2017). Policy integration and multi-level governance: dealing with the vertical dimension of policy mix designs. *Politics and Governance*, 5(2), 69–78.

Jarvis, D. S. L. (2011). *Infrastructure Regulation: What Works, Why and How Do We Know? Lessons from Asia and Beyond.* Singapore: World Scientific.

Jordan, A., Benson, D., Wurzel, R. & Zito, A. (2011). Policy instruments in practice. In J. S. Dryzek, R. B. Norgaard & D. Schlosberg, eds., *Oxford Handbook of Climate Change and Society.* Oxford: Oxford University Press, pp. 537–49.

Jordan, A., Benson, D., Wurzel, R. & Zito, A. (2012). Environmental policy: governing by multiple policy instruments? In J. J. Richardson, ed., *Constructing a Policy State? Policy Dynamics in the EU.* Oxford: Oxford University Press, pp. 105–24.

Jordan, A. & Lenschow, A. (2010). Environmental policy integration: a state of the art review. *Environmental Policy and Governance*, 20(3), 147–58.

Jordan, A. & Turnpenny, J. R. (2016). *The Tools of Policy Formulation: Actors, Capacities, Venues and Effects.* Cheltenham: Edward Elgar.

Keast, R., Mandell, M. & Brown, K. (2006). Mixing state, market and network governance modes: the role of government in "crowded" policy domains. *International Journal of Organization Theory and Behavior*, 9(1), 27–50.

Kern, F. & Howlett, M. (2009). Implementing transition management as policy reforms: a case study of the Dutch energy sector. *Policy Science*, 42(4), 391–408.

Kiss, B., Manchón, C. G. & Neij, L. (2013). The role of policy instruments in supporting the development of mineral wool insulation in Germany, Sweden and the United Kingdom. *Journal of Cleaner Production*, 48, 187–99.

Klijn, E.-H. & Koppenjan, J. F. M. (2006). Institutional design: changing institutional features of networks. *Public Management Review*, 8(1), 141–60.

Klijn, E.-H. & Koppenjan, J. (2012). Governance network theory: past, present and future. *Policy & Politics*, 40(4), 587–606.

Klijn, E. H., Koppenjan, J. & Termeer, K. (1995). Managing networks in the public sector: a theoretical study of management strategies in policy networks. *Public Administration*, 73, 437–54.

Koch, P. (2013). Overestimating the shift from government to governance: evidence from Swiss metropolitan areas. *Governance*, 26(3), 397–423

Lang, A. (2016). "Collaborative Governance in Health and Technology Policy the Use and Effects of Procedural Policy Instruments." *Administration & Society*, published online 10 August 2016. Available at https://doi.org/10.1177/0095399716664163 (last accessed 12 December, 2017.

Lascoumes, P. & Le Gales, P. (2007). Introduction: understanding public policy through its instruments – from the nature of instruments to the sociology of public policy instrumentation. *Governance*, 20(1), 1–21.

Lasswell, H. D. (1951). The policy orientation. In D. Lerner & H. D. Lasswell, eds., *The Policy Sciences: Recent Developments in Scope and Method*. Palo Alto, CA: Stanford University Press, pp. 3–15.

Latour, B. (2008). "A Cautious Prometheus? A Few Steps Toward a Philosophy of Design," Keynote Address, Networks of Design Conference, Falmouth, Cornwall, United Kingdom.

Lecuyer, O. & Quirion, P. (2013). Can uncertainty justify overlapping policy instruments to mitigate emissions? *Ecological Economics*, 93, 177–91.

Lee, Y. (2008). Design participation tactics: the challenges and new roles for designers in the co-design process. *CoDesign: International Journal of CoCreation in Design and the Arts*, 4(1), 31–50.

Levin, K., Cashore, B., Bernstein, S. & Auld, G. (2012). Overcoming the tragedy of super wicked problems: constraining our future selves to ameliorate global climate change. *Policy Sciences*, 45(2), 121–52.

Lindblom, C. E. (1959). The science of muddling through. *Public Administration Review*, 19(2), 79–88.

Linder, S. H. & Peters, B. G. (1984). From social theory to policy design. *Journal of Public Policy*, 4(3), 237–59.

Linder, S. H. & Peters, B. G. (1987). A design perspective on policy implementation: the fallacy of misplaced precision. *Review of Policy Research*, 6(3), 459–75.

Linder, S. H. & Peters, B. G. (1990). Policy formulation and the challenge of conscious design. *Evaluation and Program Planning*, 13(3), 303–11.

Linder, S. H. & Peters, B. G. (1991). The logic of public policy design: linking policy actors and plausible instruments. *Knowledge, Technology & Policy*, 4(1), 125–51.

Lowi, T. J. (1972). Four systems of politics, policy and choice. *Public Administration Review*, 32(4), 298–310.

Mahoney, J. (2012). The logic of process 'tracing tests in the social sciences. *Sociological Methods and Research*, 41(4), 566–90.

Majone, G. (1975). On the Notion of Political Feasibility. *European Journal of Political Research*, 3(2), 259–74.

May, P. J. (2003). Policy design and implementation. In B. G. Peters & J. Pierre, eds., *Handbook of Public Administration*. Beverly Hills, CA: Sage Publications, pp.223–33.

May, P. J. (2005). Regulation and compliance motivations: examining different approaches. *Public Administration Review*, 65(1), 31–44.

May, P. J. & Jochim, A. E. (2013). Policy regime perspective: policies, politics, and governing. *Policy Studies Journal*, 41(3), 426–52.

Mayntz, R. (1983). The conditions of effective public policy: a new challenge for policy analysis. *Policy and Politics*, 11(2), 123–43.

Mazey, S. & Richardson, J. (1997). Policy framing: interest groups and the lead up to 1996 Intergovernmental Conference. *West European Politics*, 20(3), 111–33.

Menahem, G. & Stein, R. (2013). High-capacity and low-capacity governance networks in welfare services delivery: a typology and empirical examination of the case of Israeli municipalities. *Public Administration*, 91(1), 211–31.

Mesequer, C. (2006). Policy learning, policy diffusion, and the making of a new order. *Annals of the American Academy*, 598, 67–82.

Meuleman, L. (2009a). The cultural dimension of metagovernance: why governance doctrines may fail. *Public Organization Review*, 10(1), 49–70.

Meuleman, L. (2009b). "Metagoverning Governance Styles: Increasing the Public Manager's Toolbox." Paper presented at the ECPR general conference, Potsdam.

Mintrom, M. & Luetjens, J. (2017). Creating public value: tightening connections between policy design and public management. *Policy Studies Journal*, 45(1), 170–90.

Moloney, K. & Stone, D., eds. (2018). *Handbook on Global Policy and Transnational Administration*. Oxford: Oxford University Press.

Mörth, U. (2000). Competing frames in the European Commission: the case of the defence of EU industry and equipment issue. *Journal of European Public Policy*, 7(2), 173–89.

Nair, S. & Howlett, M. (2017). Policy myopia as a source of policy failure: adaptation and policy learning under deep uncertainty. *Policy & Politics*, 45(1), 103-18.

Newman, J. & Head, B. W. (2017). Wicked tendencies in policy problems: rethinking the distinction between social and technical problems. *Policy and Society*, 36(3), 414-29.

O'Toole, L. J. (2014). Globalization, global governance and public administration. In S. Kim, S. Ashley, & W. H. Lambright, eds., *Public Administration in the Context of Global Governance*. Cheltenham: Edward Elgar, pp. 3-8.

Page, E. C. (2012). *Policy without Politicians: Bureaucratic Influence in Comparative Perspective*. Oxford: Oxford University Press.

Pawson, R. (2006). *Evidence-Based Policy: A Realist Perspective*. London: Sage.

Pestoff, V. A., Brandsen, T., & Verschuere, B. (2012). *New Public Governance, the Third Sector and Co-Production*. New York, NY: Routledge.

Peters, B. G. (1988). *Comparing Public Bureaucracies: Problems of Theory and Method*. Tuscaloosa, AL: University of Alabama Press.

Peters, B. G. (2014). Implementation structures as institutions. *Public Policy and Administration*, 29(2), 131-44.

Peters, B. G. (2017). What is so wicked about wicked problems? A conceptual analysis and a research program. *Policy and Society*, 36(3), 385-96.

Peters, B. G., Eliadis, P., Hill, M. M. & Howlett, M. (2005). Conclusion: the future of instruments research. In P. Eliadis, M. M. Hill, & M. J. Howlett, eds., *Designing Government: From Instruments to Governance*. Montreal, QC: McGill-Queen's University Press, pp. 353-63.

Peters, B. G. & Pierre, J. (1998). Institutions and time: problems of conceptualization and explanation. *Journal of Public Administration Research and Theory*, 8(4), 565-84.

Peters, B. G. & Tarpley, M. M. (2016). "Are Wicked Problems Really So Wicked?: Perceptions of Policy Problems." Paper presented at conference on the Governance of Wicked Problems, Wageningen, the Netherlands, 27-28 October 2016.

Pierson, P. (2004). *Politics in Time: History, Institutions, and Social Analysis*. Princeton, NJ: Princeton University Press.

Pressman, J. L. & Wildavsky, A. B. (1973). *Implementation: How Great Expectations in Washington Are Dashed in Oakland*. Berkeley, CA: University of California Press.

Pritchett, L. & Woolcock, M. (2004). Solutions when the solution is the problem: arraying the disarray in development. *World Development* (special issue: Island Studies), 32(2), 191–212.

Raadschelders, J., Vigoda-Gadot, E., & Kirsner, M., eds. (2014). *Global Dimensions of Public Administration and Governance: A Comparative Voyage.* Hoboken, NJ: Jossey-Bass.

Rayner, J., McNutt, K., & Wellstead, A. (2013). Dispersed capacity and weak coordination: the challenge of climate change adaptation in Canada's forest policy sector. *Review of Policy Research*, 30(1), 66–90.

Redström, J. (2006). Persuasive design: fringes and foundations. In A. Wijnand, I. Jsselsteijn, Y. A. W. de Kort, C. Midden, B. Eggen, & E. van den Hoven, eds., *Persuasive Technology* (Lecture Notes in Computer Science 3962). Heidelberg: Springer, pp. 112–22.

Rein, M. & Schön, D. A. (1991). Frame-reflective policy discourse. In P. Wagner, C.H. Weiss, B. Wittrock, & H. Wollman, eds., *Social Sciences and Modern States: National Experiences and Theoretical Crossroads.* Cambridge: Cambridge University Press, pp. 262–89.

Rittel, H. W. J. & Webber, M. M. (1973). Dilemmas in a general theory of planning. *Policy Sciences*, 4(2), 155–69.

Roch, C., Pitts, D., & Navarro, I. (2010). Representative bureaucracy and policy tools: ethnicity, student discipline, and representation in public schools. *Administration & Society*, 42(1), 38–65.

Rogge, K. S. & Reichardt, K. (2016). Policy mixes for sustainability transitions: an extended concept and framework for analysis. *Research Policy*, 45(8), 1620–35.

Room, G. (2011). *Complexity, Institutions and Public Policy: Agile Decision-Making in a Turbulent World.* Cheltenham: Edward Elgar.

Rotberg, R. I. (2014) Good Governance Means Performance and Results. *Governance* 27, 511–18.

Sackett, D., Rosenberg, W. M. C., Gray, J. A. M., Haynes, R. B., & Richardson, W. S. (1996). Evidence-based medicine: what it is and what it isn't. *British Medical Journal*, 312, 71–2.

Salamon, L. M. (1981). Rethinking public management: third party government and the changing forms of government action. *Public Policy*, 29(3), 255–75.

Salamon, L. M. (1989). The tools approach: basic analytics. In L. M. Salamon & M.S. Lund, eds., *Beyond Privatization: The Tools of Government Action.* Washington, DC: Urban Institute, pp. 23–50.

Salamon, L. M. (2002). *The Tools of Government: A Guide to the New Governance*. New York, NY: Oxford University Press.

Sartori, G. (1970). Concept misformation in comparative politics. *American Political Science Review*, 64(4), 1033–53.

Schneider, A. L. & Ingram, H. (1997). *Policy Design for Democracy*. Lawrence, KS: University Press of Kansas.

Schneider, A. & Sidney, M. (2009). What is next for policy design and social construction theory? *Policy Studies Journal*, 37(1): 103–19.

Schön, D. A. & Rein, M. (1994). *Frame Reflection: Solving Intractable Policy Disputes*. New York, NY: Basic Books.

Seymour-Ure, C. (1987). Institutionalization and informality in advisory systems. In W. Plowden, ed., *Advising the Rulers*. London: Blackwell Publishing, pp. 175–84.

Shore, C., Wright, S., & Pero, D., eds. (2011). *Policy Worlds: Anthropology and Analysis of Contemporary Power*. New York, NY: Berghahn Books.

Sidney, M. S. (2007). Policy formulation: design and tools. In F. Fischer, G. J. Miller, & M. S. Sidney, eds., *Handbook of Public Policy Analysis: Theory, Politics and Methods*. New Brunswick, NJ: CRC Taylor & Francis, pp. 79–87.

Simon, H. A. (1973). The structure of ill-structured problems. *Artificial Intelligence*, 4, 181–201.

Skodvin, T., Gullberg, A. T., & Aakre, S. (2010). Target-group influence and political feasibility: the case of climate policy design in Europe. *Journal of European Public Policy*, 17(6), 854–73.

Sterner, T. (2003). *Policy Instruments for Environmental and Natural Resource Management*. Washington, DC: Resource for the Future Press.

Stone, D. (2013). *Knowledge Actors and Transnational Governance: The Private-Public Policy Nexus in the Global Agora*. Houndsmill: Palgrave Macmillan.

Stone, D. & Ladi, S. (2015). Global public policy and transnational administration. *Public Administration*, 93(4), 839–55.

Swanson, D., Barg, S., Tyler, S., Venema, H., Tomar, S., Bhadwal, S., Nair, S., Roy, D., & Drexhage, J. (2010). Seven tools for creating adaptive policies. *Technological Forecasting and Social Change*, 77(6), 924–39.

Thelen, K. (2004). *How Institutions Evolve: The Political Economy of Skills in Germany, Britain, the United States, and Japan*. Cambridge: Cambridge University Press.

Thelen, K., Mahoney, J., & Rueschemeyer, D. (2003). How institutions evolve: insights from comparative historical analysis. In J. Mahoney & D. Rueschemeyer, eds., *Comparative Historical Analysis in the Social Sciences*. Cambridge: Cambridge University Press, pp. 208–40.

Thompson, J. D. & Tuden, A. (1959). *Strategy, Structure and Process in Organizational Design (Comparative Studies in Administration)*. Pittsburgh, PA: University of Pittsburgh Administrative Studies Center.

Tiernan, A. & Wanna, J. (2006). "Competence, Capacity, Capability: Towards Conceptual Clarity in the Discourse of Declining Policy Skills." Paper presented at the Govnet International Conference, Australian National University, Canberra.

Timmermans, A., Rothmayr, C., Serduelt, U., & Varone, F. (1998). "The Design of Policy Instruments: Perspectives and Concepts." Paper presented to the Midwest Political Science Association, Chicago, Illinois.

Tollefson, C., Zito, A. R., & Gale, F. (2012). Symposium overview: conceptualizing new governance arrangements. *Public Administration*, 90(1), 3–18.

Trebilcock, M. J., Tuohy, C. J., & Wolfson, A. D. (1979). "Professional regulation: a staff study of accountancy, architecture, engineering, and law in Ontario prepared for the Professional Organizations Committee." Ontario Ministry of the Attorney General.

Tribe, L. H. (1972). Policy science: analysis or ideology? *Philosophy and Public Affairs*, 2(1), 66–110.

Turnbull, N. (2017). Policy design: its enduring appeal in a complex world and how to think it differently. *Public Policy and Administration*. Published online 31 May 2017. Available at https://doi.org/10.1177/0952076717709522 (last accessed 12 December 2017).

Tunzelmann, N. von (2010). Technology and technology policy in the postwar UK: market failure or "network failure?" *Revue d'économie industrielle*, 129–130, 237–58.

Verweij, M. (2011). *Clumsy Solutions for a Wicked World: How to Improve Global Governance*. Basingstoke: Macmillan.

Walker, W. E., Marchau, V. A. W. J., & Swanson, D. (2010). Addressing deep uncertainty using adaptive policies: introduction to Section 2. *Technological Forecasting and Social Change*, 77(6), 917–23.

Warfield, J. N. & Perino Jr., G.H. (1999). The *problematique*: evolution of an idea. *Systems Research and Behavioral Science*, 16(3), 221–6.

Weaver, K. (2009a). "If You Build It, Will They Come? *Overcoming Unforeseen Obstacles to Program Effectiveness*." The Tansley Lecture, University of Saskatchewan.

Weaver, K. (2009b). *Target Compliance: The Final Frontier of Policy Implementation*. Washington, DC: Brookings Institution Press.

Weimer, D. L. (1992). The craft of policy design: can it be more than art? *Policy Studies Review*, 11(3/4), 370–88.

Weimer, D. L. (1993). The current state of design craft: borrowing, tinkering, and problem solving. *Public Administration Review*, 53(2), 110–20.

Weimer, D. L. & Vining, A. (2011). *Policy Analysis: Concepts and Practice, 5th edn*. Upper Saddle River, NJ: Pearson Prentice Hall.

Weiss, C. H. (1976). Policy research in the university: practical aid or academic exercise? *Policy Studies Journal*, 4(3): 224–8.

Whiteman, D. (1985a). The fate of policy analysis in congressional decision making: three types of use in committees." *Western Political Quarterly*, 38(2), 294–311.

Whiteman, D. (1985b). Reaffirming the importance of strategic use: a two-dimensional perspective on policy analysis in congress. *Knowledge: Creation, Diffusion, Utilization* 6(3), 203–24.

Woodside, K. (1986). Policy instruments and the study of public policy. *Canadian Journal of Political Science*, 19(4), 775–93.

Wu, X., Ramesh, M., & Howlett, M. (2015). Blending skill and resources across multiple levels of activity: competences, capabilities and the policy capacities of government. *Policy & Society*, 34(3–4), 165–71.

Wu, X., Ramesh, M., Howlett, M., & Fritzen, S. (2010). *The Public Policy Primer: Managing Public Policy*. London: Routledge.

Yi, H. & Feiock, R. C. (2012). Policy tool interactions and the adoption of state renewable portfolio standards. *Review of Policy Research*, 29(2), 193–206.

Printed in the United States
By Bookmasters